The Scotch-Irish in America

THE
SCOTCH-IRISH
IN AMERICA

SAMUEL SWETT GREEN

BooksUlster

First published by Charles Hamilton, Worcester, Mass., 1895.
This new edition published by Books Ulster. 2017.

Typographical arrangement © Books Ulster

ISBN: 978-1-910375-58-7 (Paperback)

THE SCOTCH-IRISH IN AMERICA*

Samuel Swett Green

A Paper read as the Report of the Council of the American Antiquarian Society, at the Semi-Annual Meeting, April 24, 1895, with Correspondence called out by the paper.

A TRIBUTE is due from the Puritan to the Scotch-Irishman,† and it is becoming in this Society, which has its headquarters in the heart of New England, to render that tribute.

The story of the Scotsmen who swarmed across the narrow body of water which separates Scotland from Ireland, in the seventeenth century, and who came to America in the eighteenth century, in large numbers, is of perennial interest. For hundreds of years before the beginning of the seventeenth century the Scot had been going forth continually over Europe in search of adventure and gain. As a rule, says one who knows him well, "he turned his steps where fighting was to be had, and the pay for killing was

---

* For acknowledgments regarding the sources of information contained in this paper, not made in footnotes, read the Bibliographical note at its end.

† The Scotch-Irish, as I understand the meaning of the term, are Scotch-men who emigrated to Ireland and such descendants of these emigrants as had not through intermarriage with the Irish proper, or others, lost their Scotch characteristics. Both emigrants and their descendants, if they remained long in Ireland, experienced certain changes, apart from those which are brought about by mixture of blood, through the influence of new surroundings.

reasonably good."* The English wars had made his countrymen poor, but they had also made them a nation of soldiers.

Remember the "Scotch Archers" and the "Scotch Guardsmen" of France, and the delightful story of Quentin Durward, by Sir Walter Scott. Call to mind the "Scots Brigade," which dealt such hard blows in the contest in Holland with the splendid Spanish infantry which Parma and Spinola led, and recall the pikemen of the great Gustavus. The Scots were in the vanguard of many a European host. Their activity showed itself in trade also. "In the Hanse towns and from the Baltic to the Mediterranean every busy centre and trading town knows the canny Scot."†

The adventurous spirit of the Scotsman had hitherto shown itself in war and in trade; it is now to show itself in colonization. Our interest to-day is in the colonies which Scotchmen established in the north of Ireland in the seventeenth century, and in the great emigration from those colonies to America in the eighteenth century. Large tracts of land in Ulster had been laid waste, and James the First of England formed plans for peopling them with colonies of Englishmen and Scotchmen. Hugh Montgomery, the laird of Braidstane, afterwards Lord Montgomery of the Ards, and James Hamilton, afterwards Viscount Clandeboye (a title now borne by his descendant, the Marquis of Dufferin and Ava, formerly Governor-General of Canada and Viceroy of India, who as an Irish baron is Lord Dufferin and Clandeboye), led colonies into the northern portion of County Down in 1606. About the same time plantations, which afterwards became peculiarly Scottish, were made in Antrim. Then followed what is known as the "Great plantation," in 1610. Read Scott's *Fortunes of Nigel*, it has been said, and "you see the poverty of the old land north

---

* Harrison, John. *The Scot in Ulster*, p. I.

† Macintosh in The Making of the Ulsterman, Second Scotch-Irish Congress, p. 89.

of the Tweed, and the neediness of the flock of supplicants who followed James to London." That neediness and the poverty of their land led Scotsmen to Ireland, also.

"The plantations in County Down and County Antrim, thorough as they were as far as they went, were limited in scope, in comparison with the 'Great plantation in Ulster' for which James I.'s reign will be forever remembered in Ireland."[*]

Early in the seventeenth century "all northern Ireland,—Londonderry, Donegal, Tyrone, Cavan, Armagh, and Fermanagh,— passed at one fell swoop into the hands of the crown."[†] These lands James proceeded to people with Englishmen and Scotchmen, as he had before planted Scottish and English colonies in Down and Antrim. Sir William Petty states, "that a very large emigration had taken place from Scotland after Cromwell settled the country in 1652."[‡] "He takes the total population" of Ireland in 1672 "at 1,100,000, and calculates that 800,000 were Irish, 200,000 English, and 100,000 Scots. Of course the English were scattered all over Ireland, the Scots concentrated in Ulster."[§] Lecky says that "for some years after the Revolution," meaning, of course, the English Revolution of 1688, "a steady stream of Scotch Presbyterians had poured into the country, attracted by the cheapness of the farms and by the new openings for trade."[¶] The end of the seventeenth century probably saw the last of the large emigration of Scots into Ulster.

---

[*] Harrison, p. 34.

[†] Harrison, p. 36.

[‡] *Ibid.*, p. 84.

[§] *Ibid.*, pp. 83 and 84. See, too, Petty, Sir William. *Political Survey of Ireland* in 1672, pp. 9, 18, 20 (as quoted by Harrison).

[¶] Lecky, W. E. H. *Hist. of England in the 18th Century*, Vol. II., p. 400. Amer. ed., p. 436. "In 1715 Archbishop Synge" (Synge's Letters, British Museum Add. MSS., 6, 117, p. 50) "estimated at not less than 50,000 the number of Scotch families who had settled in Ulster since the Revolution."—Lecky, p. 401. Am. ed., p. 436.

The quiet of the Scotch immigrants was disturbed by various events during the seventeenth and eighteenth centuries. War disturbed their quiet. The Irish rebellion of 1641 caused them much suffering. It "dragged its slow length along" for years, and "until Cromwell crossed in 1650, and in one dreadful campaign established the rule of the English Parliament."* The Revolution of 1688 was long and bloody, in Ireland. The sufferings of the Protestants in the north of Ireland who supported William the Third and opposed James the Second are well known, and Macaulay has rendered immortal the brave deeds of the defenders of Londonderry.†

The Scotch immigrants suffered from repression of trade and commerce. True, William III. encouraged the manufacture of linen and induced colonies of Huguenots who were driven out of France by the Revocation of the Edict of Nantes to settle in northeast Ireland. "The first blow struck" in the repression of industries, "was an Act which forbade the exportation of cattle from Ireland to England;‡ the second, when by the fifteenth of Charles II., Ireland, which up to this time in commercial matters had been held as part of England, was brought under the Navigation Acts, and her ships treated as if belonging to foreigners."§ It was in the reign of William III. that the woollen manufacture in Ireland was suppressed in the interest of the English manufacturer, and legislation which brought about this suppression was followed by "Acts forbidding the Irish to export their wool to any country save England—the English manufacturers desiring to get the wool of the sister kingdom at their own price."¶

---

* Harrison, p. 79.

† Macaulay's *History of England*, Chap. XII.

‡ Leland's *History of Ireland*, Vol. III., p. 448.

§ Harrison, p. 85. See, also, Macpherson's *History of Commerce*, Vol. III., p. 621, referred to by Harrison.

¶ *Ibid.*, p. 88. Lecky, v. 2, pp. 210 and 211. Am. ed., pp. 229 and 230.

The Scotch immigrants in Ireland were mostly Presbyterians. Under the mild ecclesiastical rule of Archbishop Usher they prospered. Later they were persecuted, and in 1704 the obnoxious Test Act was imposed by Queen Anne.

Throughout their stay in Ireland the Scotch immigrants, while they have intermarried with the Huguenots and Puritan English to a certain extent, have not intermarried with the Celtic Irish and have preserved their Scotch characteristics.[*]

It is easy to see, after the recital of facts just given, why the Scotch settlers in Ulster became discontented, and large numbers of them emigrated to America in the eighteenth century. In addition to their sufferings from the repression of trade and commerce and from religious disabilities, agriculture was in a miserable condition, and at times when land leases expired, the settlers could only renew them by paying a largely increased rent.[†]

---

[*] "Most of the great evils of Irish politics during the last two centuries have arisen from the fact that its different classes and creeds have never been really blended into one nation, that the repulsion of race or of religion has been stronger than the attraction of a common nationality, and that the full energies and intellect of the country have in consequence seldom or never been enlisted in a common cause."—Lecky, Vol. II., p. 405. Am. ed., pp.440 and 441. Travellers tell us that to-day in sections of Ulster the population is Scotch and not Irish. Honorable Leonard A. Morrison of Canobie Lake, N. H., writes me, May 8, 1895, as follows: "I am one of Scotch-Irish blood and my ancestor came with Rev. McGregor of Londonderry" (N. H.), "and neither *they* nor any of their descendants were willing to be called 'merely Irish.' I have twice visited the parish of Aghadowey, Co. Londonderry, from which they came, in Ireland, and all that locality is filled, not with 'Irish' but with Scotch-Irish, and this is pure Scotch blood to-day, after more than 200 years." Mr. Morrison is the author of a history of the Scotch-Irish town of Windham, N. H., and of several other valuable and interesting books, most of them largely genealogical.

[†] "At the time of the Revolution, when great portions of the country

The emigration to America was very striking. Some of the Scottish settlers went before 1700, and very early in the eighteenth century, but the great bulk of the emigrants came to this country at two distinct periods of time: the first, from 1718 to the middle of the century; the second, from 1771 to 1773; although there was a gentle current westward between these two eras. In consequence of the famine of 1740 and 1741, it is stated that for "several years afterwards, 12,000 emigrants annually left Ulster for the American plantations"; while from 1771 to 1773, "the whole emigration from Ulster is estimated at 30,000, of whom 10,000 are weavers."[*] August 4, 1718, there arrived in Boston five small ships containing probably about seven hundred and fifty emigrants from the north of Ireland.[†] These were nearly all Scotch-Irish. Their arrival was not unexpected, for, before coming, they had sent over a messenger to Governor Shute and been encouraged to come. A portion of the emigrants had resolved to unite in forming a settlement, and to place themselves under the pastoral care of Rev. James MacGregor, a Presbyterian minister who came over with them. Sixteen or twenty families from among these, embarked in a brigantine and sailed east in search of a suitable site for a town, the remainder going for the present to Andover and Dracut. The party in the brigantine explored a considerable

---

lay waste and when the whole framework of society was shattered, much Irish land had been let on lease at very low rents to English, and especially to Scotch Protestants. About 1717 and 1718 these leases began to fall in. Rents were usually doubled, and often trebled . . . For nearly three-quarters of a century the drain of this energetic Protestant population continued."—Lecky, Vol. 2, p. 260. Amer, ed., pp. 283, 284.

[*] Harrison, pp. 90, 91. Reid, James. *History of the Presbyterian Church in Ireland*, Ch. XXVI. Lecky, v. 2, p. 261. Am. ed., pp. 284 and 285. (Lecky refers to Killen's *Ecclesiastical History*, II., 261, 262.)

[†] Perry, Arthur L. The Scotch-Irish in New England. In Scotch-Irish in America, Second Congress, p. 109.

portion of the coast of Maine and, as cold weather came on, concluded to winter in Casco Bay at Falmouth, now Portland. They had a hard winter there and when spring came determined, with some exceptions, to seek a place of settlement with a milder and otherwise more agreeable climate. They sailed west, entered the Merrimack River and came to Haverhill. Here they heard of the town of Nutfield, now Londonderry, New Hampshire. Having examined the place, they determined to settle there. Here they were joined by the members of their party who had gone temporarily into the country, including Rev. Mr. MacGregor, and laid the foundations of a prosperous town. Londonderry grew rapidly, Scotch-Irishmen already in this country flocking to it, and emigrants of that race coming from the north of Ireland to New England generally choosing it as their place of settlement.

Another portion of the emigrants who came to Boston in 1718 went to Worcester, Massachusetts, to live. Professor Arthur L. Perry, of Williamstown, whose father was born in Worcester and whose family is one of the old families of the place, himself a descendant of one of the Scotch-Irish settlers in Worcester and an interested student of the qualities and career of that portion of the early inhabitants of the town, estimates that more than 200 Scotch-Irish people[*] went to Worcester in 1718; they probably outnumbering the population already there, who are represented as occupying fifty-eight log houses.[†]

At the time when these inhabitants went to Worcester, the people of that place were making a third attempt at settlement, they having been dispersed twice before by the Indians; and the town was not organized until September, 1722. It appears by the town records that some of the officers chosen in the earliest town

---

[*] Scotch-Irish in America, Second Congress, p. 111, comp. with p. 110.
[†] Lincoln's *History of Worcester*, p. 40 (which gives the Proprietary Records as its authority).

meetings were Scotch-Irishmen. That element of the population was not popular, however, and although the government of the Province was glad to have this addition to the number of the inhabitants of a frontier town exposed to the depredations of Indians, and although the older occupants of the place may have looked with favor at first upon the coming of the Scotch-Irish, the newcomers soon came to be disliked and were treated with marked inhospitality. They were of a different race; there was an especial prejudice against the Irish which worked to their disadvantage, although they were in reality, most of them, Scotchmen, who had merely lived in Ireland. The habits of the foreigners were different from those of the older inhabitants. They differed also in the form of their religion, and although staunch Protestants the Congregationalists, who made up the earlier settlers, were not ready to tolerate the Presbyterianism of the newcomers.

The Scotch-Irish were treated so inhospitably in Worcester that, while a considerable number of them remained there, the larger portion went away, some to Coleraine, many to Pelham;* and, after the destruction of the church they were building, many others to Western (now Warren), Blandford and other towns where they could live more comfortably and enjoy a larger liberty. They introduced the potato, so generally known in this vicinity as the Irish potato, into Worcester† as well as into Andover, Massachusetts,

---

* See, particularly for Pelham, Holland. J. G. *History of Western Massachusetts*.

† According to tradition, the potato was introduced into Worcester by one of a few families of Celtic-Irish who accompanied the Scotch-Irish when they went to Worcester. Although the potato is indigenous in the southern portion of America and was carried from this continent to Europe in the 16th century, little or nothing seems to have been known about it in New England when the band of Scotch-Irish came to Boston in 1718. Some interesting stories are told by Lincoln in his *History of Worcester* (p. 49), and by Parker in his *History of Londonderry*, N. H. (p.

and other towns and parts of the country where they settled. They are said to have made spinning fashionable in Boston.

Dr. Matthew Thornton, the distinguished New Hampshire statesman, one of the signers of the Declaration of Independence, was brought to this country by his father when only two or three years old. He received an "academical"[*] education in Worcester and after studying medicine settled down in Londonderry, New Hampshire, to practise his profession.[†] At the second annual town meeting in Worcester, held in March, 1724, James McClellan, the great-great-great Scotch-Irish grandfather of General George B. McClellan, was chosen a constable. Honorable George T. Bigelow, a former Chief Justice of the Supreme Judicial Court of Massachusetts, through his grandmother, the wife of Colonel Timothy Bigelow, a revolutionary soldier of local reputation, was descended from one of the members of the Scotch-Irish colony in Worcester. Professor Perry has also announced the discovery that the great botanist Asa Gray was a great-great-grandson of the first Scotch-Irish Matthew Gray of Worcester.

There are in Worcester to-day two old houses which are believed to have been built and occupied by the early Scotch-Irish residents, Andrew McFarland and Robert Blair.

It is an interesting fact that Abraham Blair and William Caldwell,

---

49), about the fears of early settlers of Worcester Massachusetts, that the potato was poisonous; and about ignorance of the character of the vegetable, shown by settlers in Andover in their cooking the balls of the plant instead of the tubers. See, also, Lewis's *History of Lynn*, Massachusetts, "Annals," year 1718. The potato does not seem to have been generally used in Ireland until many years after 1718. Naturally the common potato, having been introduced by emigrants from Ireland, came to be quite generally denominated the Irish potato, to distinguish it from the sweet potato. That name is used to a considerable extent to-day.

[*] Parker's *History of Londonderry*, p. 248.

[†] *Ibid.*, pp. 247, 248.

of Worcester, and several of the inhabitants of Londonderry, N. H., as survivors of the brave men who defended Londonderry, Ireland, in 1689, were, with their heirs, freed from taxation, by Act of Parliament, in British Provinces, and occupied what were here known until the Revolution as "exempt farms."

As has been related, a few of the Scotch-Irish emigrants who came to Boston in the vessels which arrived August 4, 1718, settled in Maine, a large portion went to Londonderry, N. H., and two hundred or so to Worcester. A considerable number, however, remained in Boston, and, uniting with those of their countrymen of their own faith already there, formed the religious society which was known as the Presbyterian Church in Long Lane—afterwards Federal Street. That Church became Congregational in 1786, and, on April 4, 1787, Dr. Jeremy Belknap, the founder and one of its officers until his death, of the Massachusetts Historical Society, was installed as its pastor. This is the same society which later had William Ellery Channing for its minister, and the successor to which is the Unitarian body which worships in the stone New England meeting-house on Arlington Street.

In 1719 and 1720 several hundred families of Scotch-Irish from the north of Ireland were landed on the shores of the Kennebec River in Maine in accordance with arrangements made by an Irish gentleman, Robert Temple.* They were soon dispersed by Indians and a large portion of the settlers went to Pennsylvania, and considerable numbers to Londonderry and other places. Some remained in Maine, however. This immigration is of particular interest to members of this Society, for its conductor, Robert Temple, was the ancestor of our second president, Thomas Lindall Winthrop, and his son, Robert Charles Winthrop, who has for

---

* Honorable Edward L. Pierce calls my attention to Winsor's *Memorial History of Boston*, Vol. 2, p. 540, where it is stated that our "Captain Robert Temple came over in 1717 with a number of Scotch-Irish emigrants."

so long a time taken a marked interest in our proceedings and whose loss is fresh in our memories to-day.

From 1629 to 1632 Colonel Dunbar was governor of Sagadahoc, a tract of land lying between the Kennebec and St. Croix rivers. He was a Scotch-Irishman, and made some of his countrymen large owners of land in the territory under him. They in turn introduced, in the course of two or three years, one hundred and fifty families into the territory. These were mostly Scotch-Irish, and came partly from older settlements in Massachusetts and New Hampshire and partly from Ireland. Numerous descendants of the settlers are to be found to-day in the territory which Dunbar governed, and others are scattered over the whole State of Maine.

Samuel Waldo, a member of a family well known in Boston and Worcester, was probably the last person to introduce a colony of the Scotch-Irish people into Maine prior to the Revolution. He owned large tracts of land between the Penobscot and St. George rivers. His first settlers, who went upon his lands in 1735, were Scotch-Irish, some recent immigrants, some who had been in the country since 1718. Their posterity are excellent citizens. Some of the persons wrecked in the "Grand Design" from the north of Ireland, on Mt. Desert, settled on Waldo's lands. In 1753, Samuel Waldo formed in Scotland a company of sixty adults and a number of children to settle on his possessions.

Our lamented Scotch-Irish associate, Governor Charles H. Bell, of Exeter, N. H., in the address which he made at the 150th anniversary of the settlement of old Nutfield (Londonderry), June 10, 1869, calls attention to the fact of "the prodigious increase in numbers which the descendants of the early Londonderry stock have attained, in the four or five generations which have passed away since the colony, of such slender proportions, was formed." "It is estimated," he said, "by persons best qualified to pronounce upon the subject, that the aggregate, in every section, would now fall little short of 50,000 souls."[*]

Certain it is that a large portion of the inhabitants of New Hampshire and Maine, and a considerable portion of those in Massachusetts, as well as many persons in Vermont, Rhode Island and Connecticut have had Scotch-Irish ancestors. When this people has settled in some part of our country it has sent out colonies. Parker, the historian of Londonderry, says that "during the period of twenty-five years preceding the Revolution, ten distinct settlements were made by emigrants from Londonderry, all of which have become towns of influence and importance in the State."[†]

In the first third of the seventeenth century Sir William Alexander, a favorite of James the First, tried to found a new Scotland in America. The only existing memorial of that attempt is the name of Nova Scotia.[‡] A more successful effort was made after the forced evacuation of the French from that province in 1755. About the year 1760, a party of Scotch-Irishmen, many of them from Londonderry, N. H., started a permanent settlement at Truro. Among the settlers from Londonderry were several Archibalds, members of a family which has held a distinguished place in the public life of Nova Scotia.[§] Among the pioneers was Captain William Blair also, a son of Colonel Robert Blair, of Worcester, Massachusetts, and grandson of Colonel Robert Blair, one of the defenders of Londonderry, Ireland.[¶] Other Scotch-Irish settlers followed, and their descendants became numerous, and peopled neighboring towns.

---

[*] *The Londonderry Celebration*, p. 16.

[†] Parker, Edward L. *The History of Londonderry*, p. 99.

[‡] For an account of the work done in America under the auspices of Sir William Alexander, see Proceedings and Transactions of the Royal Society of Canada, for the year 1892, Vol. X., Section 2, pp. 79–107.

[§] Parker's *Londonderry*, p. 200.

[¶] Miller, Thomas. *Historical and Genealogical Record of the first settlers of Colchester County*, etc., p. 167.

October 9, 1761, Colonel Alexander McNutt, an agent of the British government, arrived in Halifax with more than 300 settlers from the north of Ireland. In the following spring some of these went to Londonderry, Onslow, and Truro.* September 15, 1773, the "Hector," the first emigrant ship from Scotland to come to Nova Scotia, arrived in the harbor of Pictou. The pioneers who came in that vessel formed the beginning of a stream of emigrants from Scotland which flowed over the county of Pictou, the eastern portions of the province, Cape Breton, Prince Edward Island, portions of New Brunswick and even the upper provinces.† A large portion of these emigrants, however, came from the Highlands of Scotland, and, although they formed a valuable part of the population of Nova Scotia and other provinces, were of a somewhat different blood from the Lowland Scotch and their matured countrymen, the Scotch-Irish.

A very considerable portion of the people of Canada are of the Scotch-Irish race. There are in every province, it is said, centres almost entirely settled by people of that extraction. That is the case with Colchester County in Nova Scotia, in which Truro, of which I have spoken, is situated. It is so with Simcoe County in Ontario. Rev. Stuart Acheson, who was a settled pastor in the last named county for ten years, states that in his "First Essa Church"‡ all the families but one were Scotch-Irish. New Brunswick has her share of this race. It should be added, that the Counties in the Dominion of Canada in which this people have lived have been leaders in civilization.

There is an incident in Canadian history in which two distinguished Scotch-Irishmen figured conspicuously. Sir Guy Carleton, whom we remember in the United States as the

---

* Miller, p. 15.
† Patterson, George. *History of the County of Pictou, Nova Scotia*, p. 82.
‡ 3d Scotch-Irish Cong., p. 210.

Commander-in-Chief of the British Army at the close of the Revolution, was appointed Lieutenant-Governor of Quebec in 1767, and while holding that office earned for himself the title of Saviour of Canada. He was born at Strabane, in the County of Tyrone, in Ireland. Richard Montgomery, his companion in arms at the siege of Quebec when it was taken by Wolfe, was born not more than seven miles away, at Conroy.* These two

---

* This statement and several particulars of the incidents in the lives of Carleton and Montgomery given immediately after were taken from a paper entitled The Scotch-Irish in Canada, by Rev. Stuart Acheson, M.A., of Toronto, in The Scotch-Irish in America, Third Cong., pp. 195–212. John Armstrong, the writer of the life of Richard Montgomery in *The Library of American Biography*, conducted by Jared Sparks, states that Richard and his two brothers were sons of Thomas Montgomery of Conroy House. The father does not seem to have owned that place, however; it came to his son Alexander from his cousin. (See Burke's Landed Gentry [1886], Vol. II., p. 1288.) The late Mr. Henry Manners Chichester states in the article "Montgomery, Richard," in *Dictionary of National Biography*, that the latter was born at Swords, near Feltrim, Co. Dublin. One cannot help wondering whether Mr. Acheson, if he has not merely followed Armstrong or some other biographer, has not confounded Richard Montgomery with his elder brother Alexander. The suspicion arises readily because cruel acts said to have been performed in Canada by Alexander Montgomery were ascribed to Richard (see *Montcalm and Wolfe*, by Francis Parkman, Vol. II., p. 261). Of course it is not impossible that the statement of Mr. Acheson, although it may not be strictly true, leaves a correct impression, for Richard Montgomery may have spent considerable portions of his younger days with his brother at Conroy. For Richard Montgomery see, as above, Montgomery of Beaulieu, Burke's *Landed Gentry* (1886), Vol. II., p. 1288. See, also, "Ancestry of General Richard Montgomery," by Thomas H. Montgomery, in the "New York Genealogical and Biographical Record" (July, 1871), where, it is stated, his relationship to the ancestral Scottish family is traced. For Guy Carleton, see Burke's *Peerage*, under Lord Dorchester.

Scotch-Irishmen, fellow-soldiers at first, became formidable foes later. In the latter part of the year 1775, General Montgomery, as is well known, led an army of the disaffected colonies into Canada. Guy Carleton was in command of the Canadian forces which opposed him. They were both brave and able men. Montgomery had the advantage at first; he took Montreal and other places, and succeeded in placing his army between Carleton's troops and Quebec. The latter general's position seemed desperate. But he was equal to the occasion. You have often heard the story of his action at this juncture of affairs. Disguised as a French Canadian peasant or as a fisherman, with a faithful aide-de-camp also disguised, he got into a little boat to go down the St. Lawrence to Quebec. He reached Three Rivers, and found it full of the enemy. He and his companion stayed long enough in the place to take some refreshments and then, unrecognized, continued their journey. Finally they overhauled two schooners flying the British flag,

---

It is very difficult to be perfectly accurate, with information now readily accessible, in respect to statements regarding the Scotch-Irish, and it is evident that men who came from the north of Ireland, or descendants from such persons, have been not infrequently claimed as of Scotch extraction, without sufficient investigation, and when they had but little Scotch blood. Many of the Presbyterians of the north of Ireland were of Huguenot, Welsh, English, and other extractions. I have taken reasonable pains to be accurate, but cannot hope that I have been perfectly so. Two things are evident, however, namely, that very large numbers of emigrants from Ireland of Scotch blood came to this country in the 18th century, and that they exerted a great influence here for good, particularly in the Southern Middle and Southern Atlantic States. It may also be added, without disparagement of the good qualities of men of other extractions, that the powerful and beneficent influence which they exerted was largely the result of peculiarly Scottish characteristics. It is also not improbable that many persons without Scotch blood in their veins came from being trained in childhood and boyhood in Scotch communities, to have what we recognize as Scotch characteristics.

were taken aboard and carried to Quebec. Montgomery united with Benedict Arnold, who had made a futile attempt to take the citadel of Quebec, at Pointe aux Trembles and, together, they proceeded to make another attempt to take Quebec. They reached the Plains of Abraham, and demanded its surrender. Carleton declined to surrender. After battering the walls of the citadel for a short time ineffectually, Montgomery determined to storm the town. You recall the failure of the attempt, and the tragic end of Montgomery. As he and his men came under the fire of the enemy its cannon greeted them with a destructive discharge, and the brave general and many of his men were laid low in death.* After the battle Carleton sought out, amid the winter snow, the body of his fellow-countryman and neighbor, and, paying the tribute of one Scotch-Irishman to another Scotch-Irishman, had it buried with military honors.

In 1682, William Penn interested a number of prominent Scotchmen in a scheme for colonizing the eastern section of New Jersey. "These Scotchmen," says Douglas Campbell, "sent over a number of settlers who have largely given character to this sturdy little State, not the least of their achievements being the building-up, if not the nominal founding, of Princeton College, which has contributed so largely to the scholarship of America."†

While considerable numbers of the Scotch-Irish emigrated to New England in the great exodus from Ireland during the fifty or sixty years prior to the American Revolution, the great body of those coming here entered the continent by way of Philadelphia.

---

* Scotch-Irish in America, Third Cong., p. 202. (Paper by Stuart Acheson.) The writer would seem to have been mistaken in supposing that Montgomery was killed by shot fired from the guns of Fort Diamond on the summit of the citadel.

† Baird, Rev. Robert, *Religion in the United States of America*, p. 154, as referred to by Campbell, Vol. II., p. 484.

Penn's Colony was more hospitable to immigrants of faiths differing from the prevalent belief of its inhabitants, than were most of the New England provinces.

Then, too, the Scotch-Irish emigrants were mostly farmers, and did not find New England so favorable from an agricultural point of view as some of the middle and southern colonies.

Immigrants came in such numbers to Philadelphia as to frighten James Logan, the Scotch-Irish[*] Quaker Governor of Pennsylvania from 1699 to 1749. He complains in 1725 that "it looks as if Ireland were to send all her inhabitants hither; if they will continue to come, they will make themselves proprietors of the province."[†] The bold stream of settlers who came to Philadelphia, flowed westward and occupied considerable portions of the province of Pennsylvania.

It is said of Pittsburg that it is Scotch-Irish in "substantial origin, in complexion and history,—Scotch-Irish in the countenances of the living and the records of the dead."[‡]

It is estimated that at the time of the Revolution one-third of the population of Pennsylvania was Scotch-Irish.

A large portion of the emigrants who came from the north of Ireland to Philadelphia, went south. This was especially the case after Braddock's defeat in 1755, made the Indians bold and agressive in the west.

A very large portion of the people in the South Atlantic States are of Scotch-Irish extraction.

During many years of the eighteenth century a stream of

---

[*] Professor George Macloskie in Scotch-Irish in America, Third Cong., p. 97.

[†] Macloskie, in First Scotch-Irish Congress, p. 95. Professor Macloskie speaks of Logan as a Scotch-Irish Quaker who was "a native of County Armagh, Ireland."

[‡] The Scotch-Irish in Western Pennsylvania. John Dalzell, in Second Scotch-Irish Congress, p. 175.

emigrants flowed south, through Maryland, Virginia, North Carolina, South Carolina, and across the Savannah river, into Georgia. Their movements were parallel with the lines of the Blue Ridge.

In Maryland they settled, mainly, in the narrow slip of land in the western part of the State, although they were to be found scattered through all portions of the province.

In the latter part of the seventeenth and the earlier years of the eighteenth centuries there were many Scotch-Irish residents in Virginia, east of the Blue Ridge mountains; some were even settled west of that range. In 1738 began a movement which completely filled the valley west of the Blue Ridge, from Pennsylvania to North Carolina, with men of that race, excepting the lower portion, which was occupied by Germans.

In the year 1736, Henry McCulloch, from the province of Ulster, obtained a grant of 64,000 acres in the present County of Duplin, North Carolina, and introduced upon it between three and four thousand of his Scotch-Irish countrymen from the north of Ireland.

Besides the large number of emigrants of this nationality who came, through Virginia from Pennsylvania, into North Carolina, many ships filled with Scotch-Irish passengers from the north of Ireland came into Charleston and other southern ports, and the emigrants moving north met those coming south from Pennsylvania and settled with them in North Carolina and other southern States.

Our associate, William Wirt Henry, in speaking of the Scotch-Irish, says: "So great was the population of the race in North Carolina before the Revolution, that they may be said to have given direction to her history. With their advent, began the educational history of the State."*

---

* The Scotch-Irish of the South, by William Wirt Henry, in First Scotch-

Dr. David Ramsay, an ardent patriot in Revolutionary times, like the New Hampshire physician, Matthew Thornton, wrote much, as is well known, about the history of South Carolina. He says, as quoted by Henry, in speaking of pre-revolutionary times, that "scarce a ship sailed from any of 'the ports of Ireland' for Charleston, that was not crowded with men, women, and children." He speaks, too, of a thousand emigrants who came in a single year from Pennsylvania and Virginia, driving their horses, cattle and hogs before them and who were assigned places in the western woods of the province. These, says Henry, were Scotch-Irish. They were distinguished by economy and industry, and the portion of the province occupied by them soon became its most populous part.

Ramsay says, that to this element in the population, "South Carolina is indebted for much of its early literature. A great proportion of its physicians, clergymen, lawyers and schoolmasters were from North Britain."[*]

The early settlers of South Carolina were largely Huguenots; the province seems to have been generously peopled, too, by the Scotch-Irish, a race which was connected by a religious tie to the Huguenots, both being warm Calvinists.

The prosperity of Georgia has been largely owing to Scotch-Irish settlers and their descendants.

The pioneers of Kentucky were mainly from Virginia and North Carolina, and its population is largely Scotch-Irish in its ancestry. The first settlers of Tennessee crossed over the mountains from North Carolina and with subsequent emigrants made that State one of those, a very large portion of whose people are of the same race. Mississippi and Alabama, Florida, Arkansas and Missouri, were settled at first by emigrants from adjacent States and have

---

Irish Congress, pp. 123, 124.

[*] Ramsay as quoted by Henry, First Cong. of the Scotch-Irish, p. 125.

all of them, naturally, a considerable Scotch-Irish element in their population.

Texas was conquered by a Scotch-Irishman, General Sam Houston,* and has many families of Scotch-Irish ancestry within its borders. There are many representatives of this race in other States, such as Ohio, Iowa, Minnesota and California. The race has been prolific and, being of a hardy, brave and adventurous spirit, has gone everywhere throughout the country.

The story of Cherry Valley, a little town in New York that was settled by Scotch-Irishmen in 1741, is very interesting, but I have no time to tell it.†

The Scotch-Irish settlers who came to this country repaired, for the most part, to the frontiers of the colonies. This is true of those who went to the Middle and South Atlantic States, where they were found mainly in their western portions. It was true, also, of such as came to Maine, to Londonderry, New Hampshire, and to Worcester, Massachusetts. The result was that it was in very large measure people of this nationality who were engaged in the Indian struggles which preceded the Revolution.

We find men of this race actively engaged in the Old French war, which began in 1744, and in the later contest between Great

---

* "His" (Houston's) "ancestors on his father's and mother's side are traced back to the Highlands of Scotland." They emigrated to the north of Ireland. "Here they remained until the siege of Derry, in which they were engaged, when they emigrated to Pennsylvania."—D. C. Kelley in Scotch-Irish in America, Second Congress, p. 145.

† From this town came the ancestors of the late Douglas Campbell, a descendant of one of the defenders of Londonderry, Ireland, whose recently published work, *The Puritan in England, Holland and America*, has attracted considerable attention. The last chapter of his volumes is an interesting summary of much that has become known about the Scotch-Irish in the United States.—See Campbell, Vol. II., p. 482, note. American Ancestry. (J. Munsell's Sons.) Vol. 8, 1893, p. 156.

Britain and France on this continent, upon the renewal of hostilities in 1756. Thus, soldiers from Londonderry served under Pepperell in the expedition against Cape Breton. During the later attempt upon Crown Point, three companies of hardy men, who had adroitness in traversing woods, were selected from the New Hampshire regiment to act as rangers. Many of the men selected were from the Scotch-Irish town of Londonderry, and the three captains, Robert Rogers, John Stark, and William Stark, had all been residents of the same place. The two latter were brothers and sons of an early Scotch-Irish inhabitant of the town.* Rogers, a brave and skilful officer, was soon made Major, and his body of rangers performed active and efficient service. A company of soldiers from Londonderry aided in the reduction of Canada in the campaign when Quebec was taken by Wolfe.

In the Colonial wars which preceded the Revolution, it is stated that the soldiers of Virginia were principally drawn rom the Scotch-Irish settlements in the valley west of the Blue Ridge and in the Piedmont Counties. Previous to the encounter at Lexington, three British soldiers deserted from the army in Boston and found their way to Londonderry. Their hiding place was disclosed and a detachment of soldiers was sent from Boston to arrest them. They were taken prisoners, but had not gone far before a company of young men, which had been hurriedly raised in Londonderry, by Captain James Aiken, caught up with their captors and demanded and secured their release. The rescued men afterwards lived unmolested in Londonderry.† As soon as the news of the battle of Lexington reached New Hampshire, 1200 troops immediately

---

* Parker (p. 239) says that Archibald Stark, the father of William and John Stark, was, like many of the early emigrants to Londonderry, N. H., "a native of Scotland, and emigrated while young to Londonderry in Ireland."

† Parker, p. 104.

repaired to Cambridge and Charlestown. Among these was a large company from Londonderry, commanded by George Reed, who upon the organization of the troops at Cambridge was made a Colonel. The New Hampshire Convention held at Exeter, April 25, 1775, formed the troops of that State then near Boston, into two regiments under the command of Colonels Reed and Stark, natives of Londonderry.

At the first call of Congress for soldiers to defend Boston, Daniel Morgan, of Scotch-Irish blood,[*] immediately raised a company of riflemen among his people in the lower valley of Virginia, and by a forced march of six hundred miles reached the beleaguered town in three weeks.

The back or upper counties of Virginia were Scotch-Irish. Their representatives got control of the House of Burgesses, and it was by their votes, and under the leadership of the young Scotchman,[†] Patrick Henry, that were passed, in opposition to the combined efforts of the old leaders of the province, those resolutions denying the validity of the Stamp Act, which roused the continent.[‡]

While it cannot be allowed that the Scotch-Irish people of Mecklenburg county, North Carolina, passed resolutions May 20, 1775, declaring their independence of Great Britain, it is certain that on the 31st of that month they uttered patriotic sentiments fully abreast of the time.[§]

The men of this race showed these sentiments everywhere

---

[*] W. W. Henry, in Scotch-Irish in America, First Cong., p. 118.

[†] William Wirt Henry writes in the article "Henry, Patrick," in Appleton's *Cyclopædia of American Biography*, of Patrick Henry: "His father, John Henry, was a Scotchman, son of Alexander Henry and Jean Robertson, a cousin of the historian William Robertson and of the mother of Lord Brougham."

[‡] Henry in First Scotch-Irish Cong., p. 118.

[§] *Narrative and Critical History of America*, Ed. by Justin Winsor, v. 6, pp. 256, 257, note.

throughout the Colonies. Four months before the passage of the resolutions in Mecklenburg County, the freeholders of Fincastle County, Virginia, presented an address to the Continental Congress in which they declared, that if an attempt were made to dragoon them out of the privileges to which they were entitled as subjects of Great Britain and to reduce them to slavery, they were "deliberately and resolutely determined never to surrender them to any power on earth but at the expense of" their "lives."[*]

It was seventeen days before the Declaration of Independence that eighty-three able-bodied men of the Scotch-Irish town of Peterborough, N. H., signed this resolution:

"We, the subscribers, do hereby solemnly engage and promise, that we will, to the utmost of our power, at the risk of our lives and fortune, with arms, oppose the hostile proceedings of the British fleets and armies against the united Colonies."[†]

It has been suggested that even after the Declaration of Independence had been adopted by Congress, it would not have been signed and promulgated but for the action of John Witherspoon, one of the delegates from New Jersey, the President of Princeton College, a Scotch Presbyterian clergyman and a descendant of John Knox. Seeing how the other representatives held back, he rose in his place, you remember, and declaring that as his gray head must soon bow to the fate of all, he preferred that it should go by the axe of the executioner rather than that the cause of independence should not prevail.[‡]

Several Scotchmen and Scotch-Irishmen signed the Declaration.

---

[*] Professor Henry Alexander White, in Scotch-Irish in America, Second Cong., p. 232.

[†] Parker, p. 186.

[‡] This anecdote appears in a number of places. (See, *e. g.*, Craighead's *Scotch and Irish Seeds*, etc., p. 334.) It may be found with the particular turn given to it here in The Scotch-Irish in America, First Cong., pp. 182, 183, in an address by Colonel A. K. M'Clure, of Philadelphia.

Professor Macloskie, a Scotch-Irish professor in Princeton College, states that the "Declaration of Independence as we have it to-day is in the handwriting of a Scotch-Irishman, Charles Thomson, the Secretary of Congress; was first printed by Captain Thomas Dunlap, another Scotch-Irishman, who published the first daily newspaper in America; a third Scotch-Irishman, Captain John Nixon, of Philadelphia, first read it to the people."*

The Scotch-Irish came to this country full of bitter feeling towards the government of Great Britain. They had been oppressed by that government and they believed that it had wickedly broken faith with them. They hated, too, the hierarchy of the Church of England. Presbyterians as they were, they had been oppressed by that hierarchy. They sympathized, also, with the Puritans of New England, who regarded the presence here of bishops and other ecclesiastics of the Church of England as the presence of the emissaries of a foreign power that was trying to reduce them to subjection.

It was largely through Scotch-Irish influence and support that religious liberty was established in Virginia and elsewhere throughout this country. These showed themselves when, in 1776, Patrick Henry, a Scotchman, as before stated, led in the movement which secured the insertion in the famous Bill of Rights of Virginia of the declaration that one of the inalienable rights of man is his right to worship God according to the dictates of his conscience.

It was through the pressure of Scotch-Irish Presbyterians that Jefferson, in the next session of the assembly, was prompted to write, and by their votes that he secured the passage of, the act for the establishment of religious liberty, which has done so much to

---

* Professor George Macloskie, Princeton College, to whom Campbell declares himself indebted for the information given. See Campbell, Vol. II., p. 487 (note). See, also, The Scotch-Irish in America, First Congress, p. 95.

effect the divorce of Church and State in Virginia and throughout the Union.

In contemplating the wide-reaching results of the example set here in America, Mr. William Wirt Henry is led to add to a statement similar to the one just made, "Thus there was completed by the Scotch-Irish in Virginia, in 1776, the Reformation commenced by Luther two hundred and fifty years before."[*]

The Scotch-Irish, as you would imply from what I have said before, entered into the contest of the Revolution, not only to uphold civil and religious liberty, but also with a zeal inspired by an ardent desire to pay off old scores.[†] The Scotch-Irish served in great numbers in the Continental array and in the militia of the several States during the Revolution, and the achievements of their officers and men were often brilliant. When the British landed at Charlestown "the two New Hampshire regiments were ordered to join the forces on Breed's Hill. A part were detached to throw up a work on Bunker Hill, and the remainder under" the Colonels born in Londonderry, "Stark and Reed, joined the Connecticut forces under General Putnam, and the regiment of Colonel Prescott, at the rail-fence. 'This was the very point of the British attack, the key of the American position.'"[‡]

Again, it was John Stark who hurriedly gathered together 1,400 well-trained militia from New Hampshire and Vermont, and instead of making Molly Stark a widow, beat the detachment

---

[*] Scotch-Irish in America, First Cong., p. 123.

[†] Froude says: "But throughout the revolted colonies, and, therefore, probably in the first to begin the struggle, all evidence shows that the foremost, the most irreconcilable, the most determined in pushing the quarrel to the last extremity, were the Scotch-Irish whom the bishops and Lord Donegal and Company had been pleased to drive out of Ulster."—*The English in Ireland in the 18th Century*, by J. A. Froude, Vol. II., p. 141 (English ed.).

[‡] Parker, p. 106.

of troops which Burgoyne had sent to Bennington, giving the Americans the much needed inspiration of a victory. In less than two months followed the battle of Saratoga, October 7, 1777. Burgoyne was conducting an armed reconnoissance and much fighting ensued. The right of the British line was commanded by the brave Scotchman, General Simon Fraser. On the left of the American troops was the equally brave Scotch-Irish Colonel Morgan, with his regiment of sharpshooters. The Scotch-Irish in America were generally fine marksmen.* Seeing that an officer on an iron gray charger was active in the fight and that wherever he went he turned the tide of battle, Morgan, calling to some of the best men in his regiment, pointed to the officer and said, "Bring him down." At the crack of a faithful rifle the gallant British officer reeled in his saddle and fell. That officer was Simon Fraser, the idol of Burgoyne's army.† Burgoyne was now in straits, and failing to receive hoped-for aid from Sir Henry Clinton, surrendered his army on the 17th of the month.

A distinguished member of this Society‡ has labored hard, during the last few years, in forcible and eloquent speech, to secure for the pioneer settler of the Northwestern Territory, General Rufus Putman, of Rutland, Massachusetts, due recognition of what he regards as his great merits as an officer in the Revolutionary army, and his inestimable services in giving a proper tone to the settlements in the northwest. It is interesting to

---

* Parker quotes from an unnamed writer the following words as written about the troops under Colonels Stark and Reed at Bunker Hill: "Almost every soldier equalled William Tell as a marksman, and could aim his weapon at an opposer with as keen a relish. Those from the frontiers had gained this address against the savages and beasts of the forests."—Parker's *History of Londonderry*, p. 106.
† William Wirt Henry in First Scotch-Irish Congress, p. 119. Lossing's *Pictorial Field Book of the Revolution*, Vol. I., p. 62.
‡ Hon. George F. Hoar.

mention in connection with this fact another fact, namely, that the Northwestern Territory, then claimed by Virginia, was taken possession of in 1778, in an ever memorable campaign, by the great soldier, Colonel George Rogers Clark, of Scotch descent,* and two hundred brave men of the Scotch-Irish race whom he had collected for his secret expedition, in Augusta County, Virginia, and in Kentucky, at the command of the Scotch governor, Patrick Henry.

It would be a pleasant task to speak at length of the exploits, during the Revolution, of officers and men from the Middle and Southern States, of Scotch-Irish extraction, for a majority of the troops who served on the American side, from Pennsylvania and the States south of it, seem to have been of that nationality. I can only mention, however, the battle of King's Mountain, which was fought by a body of troops composed of Huguenots and of Scotch-Irish volunteers. This battle took place the 7th of October, 1780, just three years after the memorable engagement at Saratoga, and, like the earlier contest, was a turning point in the affairs of the Americans. That battle was the forerunner of the surrender

---

* Mr. Reuben G. Thwaites, Secretary of The State Historical Society of Wisconsin, writes to the author of this paper, as follows:—"According to all family traditions, John Clark, great-grandfather of George Rogers Clark, came to Virginia in 1630, from the southwest part of Scotland. According to one tradition, a few years later, he visited friends in Maryland, and married there 'a red-haired Scotch woman.' George Rogers Clark himself, had 'sandy' hair; another tradition has it, that the woman was a Dane. Their one son, William John, died early, leaving two sons, John(²) and Jonathan. Jonathan was a bachelor, and left his estate to his brother's son, John(³). One of William John's daughters married a Scotch settler, McCloud, and their daughter married John Rogers, father of the Ann Rogers who married John Clark(⁴), her cousin, and thus she became the mother of George Rogers Clark. So George Rogers Clark had Scotch ancestry on both sides of the house."

of Cornwallis at Yorktown, and stood in causal relations to it, just as the battle of Saratoga resulted in the capture of the army of Burgoyne.

Besides the officers already mentioned, the Scotch-Irish contributed to the Continental array during the Revolution such men as General Henry Knox of Massachusetts,[*] General George Clinton of New York,[†] and, as claimed on apparently good grounds, Colonel John Eager Howard of Maryland, who changed the fortunes of the day at the battle of Cowpens, Colonel William Campbell of Virginia, who won the battle of King's Mountain, and General Andrew Pickens of South Carolina.[‡]

---

[*] See *Life and Correspondence of Henry Knox*, etc., by Francis S. Drake, Boston, 1873, pp. 8, 9.

[†] *American Ancestry*, Vol. VI., 1891, p. 52.

[‡] General Anthony Wayne, the brave hero of Stony Point, is commonly spoken of as a Scotch-Irishman. His father was born in Wicklow County, Ireland. There was a tradition in the family that the Waynes were of Welsh origin. They may have intermarried with persons of Scotch blood, however. (See *American Ancestry,* Vol. IV., p. 75.) General John Sullivan of Maine and New Hampshire, older brother of Governor James Sullivan of Massachusetts, is sometimes claimed as a Scotch-Irishman. He certainly was Irish, but I do not find that he was Scotch also. In Craighead's *Scotch and Irish Seeds in American Soil*, Rev. Dr. Smith is quoted as saying that General Morgan, the hero of Cowpens, and General Pickens, who made the arrangements for that battle, were "both Presbyterian elders," and that "nearly all under their command were Presbyterians." (p. 312.) Dr. Smith is also quoted as saying, that "in the battle of King's Mountain, Colonel Campbell" and several other high officers were Presbyterian elders, and that "the body of their troops were collected from Presbyterian settlements." (p. 342.) General Wayne is mentioned as a Presbyterian, (p. 340.) Of course there were many Presbyterians not of Scotch or Scotch-Irish blood, but men of those races who emigrated to America and their families were for the most part of that denomination. The picturesque Kentuckian, Daniel Boone, is often spoken of as a Scotch-Irishman. It

"After the adoption of the Declaration of Independence, the various States proceeded to form their independent governments. Then the Scotch-Irish gave to New York her first governor, George Clinton, who filled the position for seven terms, of three years each, and died during his second term of office as Vice-President of the United States. To Delaware they gave her first governor, John MacKinney. To Pennsylvania they gave her war governor, Thomas McKean, one of the signers of the Declaration of Independence. To New Jersey Scotland gave her war governor, William Livingston, and to Virginia, Patrick Henry, not only her great war governor" but her civil leader.*

"It is a noteworthy fact in American history," writes Douglas Campbell, "that of the four members of Washington's cabinet, Knox, of Massachusetts, the only New Englander, was a Scotch-Irishman; Alexander Hamilton of New York was a Scotch-Frenchman; Thomas Jefferson was of Welsh descent; and the fourth, Edmund Randolph, claimed among his ancestors the Scotch Earls of Murray. New York also furnished the first Chief Justice of the United States, John Jay, who was a descendant of French Huguenots; while the second Chief Justice, John Rutledge, was Scotch-Irish, as were also Wilson and Iredell, two of the four original associate justices; a third, Blair, being of Scotch origin. John Marshall, the great Chief Justice, was, like Jefferson, of Welsh descent."†

After the formation of the United States government we find

---

is well known that the late Lyman C. Draper had unusual facilities for finding out the truth in regard to the Boones. Mr. Reuben G. Thwaites writes me from Madison, Wisconsin, as follows: "Daniel Boone's father was of pure English stock, from Devonshire; his mother, Sarah Morgan, was a Welsh Quaker. Draper's notes clearly indicate that he discarded the Scotch-Irish theory regarding Sarah."

* Campbell, Vol. II., p. 487.

† *Ibid.*, p. 481, note.

men of the Scotch-Irish race winning honors in war as they had done in the Revolution, and in the earlier contests between France and Great Britain, and with the North American Indians.

At first, the United States had only a nominal army. In the spring of 1792 the number of troops was increased to 5,000, a legionary organization was adopted, and Anthony Wayne was appointed Major-General. With this army General Wayne took the field against the Miami Indians, and overthrew them at the battle of Maumee Rapids on August 20, 1794.

You all remember the stirring picture of the Battle of Lake Erie in the Capitol at Washington. Commodore Oliver Hazard Perry, taking his younger brother Alexander with him and calling to four sailors to row him to the *Niagara*, is represented, with the flag of his vessel wrapped around his arm, as he passed from the disabled *Lawrence* in a small boat to the ship next in size to the ruined flag-ship. Going out from Put-in-Bay the 10th of September, 1813, with his whole squadron, he met the British fleet in a memorable naval contest. Himself a young man of twenty-eight years of age he was opposed to one of Nelson's veterans. Himself a Scotch-Irishman, his opponent, Captain Robert H. Barclay, was a Scotchman. The engagement was hot, but at three o'clock in the afternoon the gallant Perry saw the British flag hauled down. For the first time since she had created a navy, Great Britain lost an entire squadron. "We have met the enemy and they are ours," is the familiar line in which Perry announced his victory, in a despatch to General William Henry Harrison. Commodore Perry's mother was Sarah Wallace Alexander, a Scotch woman from the north of Ireland.* She became the mother of five sons, all of whom

---

* Christopher Raymond Perry, the father of Oliver Hazard Perry, met his future wife when confined as a prisoner of war at Newry, Ireland. She was a granddaughter of "James Wallace, an officer in the Scotch army and a signer of the Solemn League and Covenant" who "fled in

were officers in the United States Navy. Two daughters married Captain George W. Rogers and Dr. William Butler of the U. S. Navy. Dr. Butler was the father of Senator Matthew Calbraith Butler, of South Carolina. After the victory at Lake Erie, some farmers in Rhode Island, you remember, declared, such was the estimation in which they held this woman, that it was "Mrs. Perry's victory."*

The furious battle at the Horse Shoe of the Tallapoosa River with the Creek Indians, March 27, 1814, brought to the front General Sam Houston, a man of the Scotch-Irish race of whom the country has heard much. Major-General Andrew Jackson, another distinguished Scotch-Irishman,[†] commanded in that battle. Jackson's father, also named Andrew, came from Carrickfergus, on the north coast of Ireland, in 1765. This battle was a signal victory, and soon after a treaty of peace was signed by which the hostile Creeks lost the greater part of their territory. It is unnecessary to

---

1660 with others, from County Ayr to the north of Ireland."—Our Naval Heroes, by D. C. Kelley, in The Scotch-Irish in America, Fifth Congress, p. 115. See, also, "Ancestry of thirty-three Rhode Islanders," &c., by John Osborne Austin, under Perry.

* Our Naval Heroes, by D. C. Kelley, in Fifth Scotch-Irish Congress, pp. 114–116. See Lossing's *Pictorial Field Book of the War of 1812*, Ch. 25.

† Among other places see Andrew Jackson, by D. C. Kelley, in Scotch-Irish in America, Third Congress, p. 182. Andrew Jackson as a Public Man, by William Graham Sumner (American Statesmen Series), Boston: 1882. James Parton in his life of Andrew Jackson says (pp. 17 and 48, vol. 1): "I may as well remark here as anywhere, that the features and shape of head of General Jackson, which ten thousand sign-boards have made familiar to the people of the United States, are common in North Carolina and Tennessee. In the course of a two months' tour in those States among the people of Scotch-Irish descent, I saw more than twenty well-marked specimens of the long, slender Jacksonian head, with the bushy, bristling hair, and the well known features."

speak of General Jackson's success at New Orleans in January of the following year.

It must be stated, however, that General James Miller, who won universal admiration by his gallant attack upon a battery at Lundy's Lane, July 25, 1814, was Scotch-Irish, a native of Peterborough and out of the loins of Londonderry.* It is he who was subsequently Collector of Customs at Salem for more than twenty years, and of whom Hawthorne speaks so enthusiastically, calling him "New England's most distinguished soldier."†

Zachary Taylor, the popular hero of the Mexican war, is generally reckoned as having been of Scotch-Irish extraction; of that race, too, of course, was Matthew Calbraith Perry, the brother of the victor of the battle of Lake Erie, who ably assisted Scott as a naval commander at Vera Cruz, and who afterwards organized and conducted with marked success the well known expedition to Japan.

Officers and men of the Scotch-Irish race served in large numbers on both sides in the late Civil War, but I cannot stop to mention even the names of the most distinguished.

Mr. Campbell says "of the twenty-three Presidents of the United States, the Scotch-Irish have contributed six—Jackson, Polk, Taylor, Buchanan, Johnson, Arthur; the Scotch three—Monroe, Grant, Hayes; the Welsh one—Jefferson; and the Hollanders one—Van Buren. Garfield's ancestors on his father's side came from England, but the family line is traced back into Wales; his mother was a French Huguenot. Cleveland's mother was Irish;

---

* See in *History of the town of Peterborough*, N. H., by Albert Smith, Genealogy and history of Peterborough families," p. 147. In the sketch of General Miller in Smith's history is a letter to his wife Ruth, written from Fort Erie, July 28, 1814, three days after the battle of Lundy's Lane.
† "The Custom House," introductory to the *Scarlet Letter*.

Benjamin Harrison's mother was Scotch."* "The pedigrees of Madison and Lincoln are doubtful."[†]

Six of the early settlers of the Scotch-Irish town of Londonderry, or their descendants, writes Parker, "have filled the gubernatorial chair of New Hampshire, namely, Matthew Thornton, who was President of the Provincial Congress, in 1775, Jeremiah Smith, Samuel Bell, John Bell, Samuel Dinsmore, and Samuel Dinsmore, Jr."[‡] To these names must be added at least one more, namely, that of our late associate, Governor and United States Senator, Charles Henry Bell, of Exeter, who was the third chief magistrate of New Hampshire, bearing the surname of the ancestor of the three, John Bell of Londonderry, N. H. Our late associate John James Bell, grandson of Governor Samuel Bell and son of Judge Samuel D. Bell, and Hon. Luther V. Bell, formerly Superintendent of the McLean Asylum, Somerville, Massachusetts, were also descendants of John Bell of Londonderry.

The Rev. Dr. Joseph MacKean, first President of Bowdoin College, was a native of Londonderry.[§]

The venerable Rev. Dr. John H. Morison, of Boston, is of Scotch-Irish extraction and is descended from the father of the first male child born in Londonderry. It is of him that the story is told that after he had delivered an election sermon before the

---

* Campbell, Vol. 2, p. 493, note.

† *Ibid.* The writer of this paper has not studied the pedigrees of the presidents, but gives the statement made regarding the above as that of an investigator who, while not by any means free from mistakes, is pretty careful in respect to assertions. The same remark should be made regarding some of the other pedigrees contained in other extracts from Mr. Campbell's *History*.

‡ Parker, p. 208.

§ His father, John MacKean, was born April 13, 1715, at Ballymoney, in the County of Antrim, Ireland, and was about four years of age when his father emigrated to this country.—Parker, p. 224.

New Hampshire legislature, and it had been moved to print a certain number of copies of the discourse, a member rose and said that he would move that additional copies be printed if the brogue of the preacher could be reproduced.

Horace Greeley, according to Whitelaw Reid, was of Scotch-Irish ancestry on both sides of his house.*

John Caldwell Calhoun, the great Southern statesman, like his sturdy opponent, President Jackson, was of the Scotch-Irish race,† so were the great inventors, Robert Fulton,‡ Cyrus H. McCormick,§ and Samuel Finley Breese Morse. The last named

---

* See "Greeley, Horace," written by Whitelaw Reid, in Appleton's *Cyclopædia of American Biography*.

† John C. Calhoun was the grandson of James Calhoun, who is said to have emigrated from Donegal, Ireland, in 1733 (*John C. Calhoun*, by Dr. H. von Holst, p. 8.) John C. Calhoun was the son of Patrick Calhoun, whom James Parton, in his *Famous Americans of Recent Times* speaks of (pp. 117, 118) as a Scotch-Irishman, who, with Andrew Jackson and Andrew Johnson, other Scotch-Irishmen, illustrates well the "North of Ireland" character. Patrick Calhoun was a Presbyterian like his father (J. Randolph Tucker, in article "Calhoun, John Caldwell" in Appleton's *Cyclopædia of American Biography*). In 1770, Patrick Calhoun (von Holst, p. 8,) married Martha Caldwell, who, says John S. Jenkins in his *Life of John Caldwell Calhoun* (p. 21), was a daughter of a Scotch-Irish Presbyterian, who, according to Tucker, was an emigrant from Ireland.

‡ "Robert Fulton was born in Little Britain, Lancaster Co., Pa., 1765. He was of respectable though not wealthy family. His father and mother were of Scotch-Irish blood. Their families were supposed to be a part of the great emigration from Ireland in 1730–31. The Fulton family were probably among the early settlers of the town of Lancaster, as the father of Robert Fulton was one of the founders of the Presbyterian Church of that place."—The Inventors of the Scotch-Irish race, by J. H. Bryson, in The Scotch-Irish in America, Fourth Congress, p. 175.

§ Scotch-Irish in America, First Congress, p. 101, Fourth Congress, p. 185.

was the son of our late associate Rev. Jedidiah Morse, and the great-grandson of Rev. Dr. Samuel Finley, a Scotch-Irish President of Princeton* College. The celebrated surgeon, Dr. D. Hayes Agnew, was Scotch-Irish on both sides of his family.[†] Joseph Henry was of Scotch descent.[‡] Alexander Graham Bell, the inventor of the telephone, is a native of Scotland.[§] In Canada the distinguished statesman Robert Baldwin and a large portion of his associates in securing the establishment of the Dominion of Canada are stated to have been of Scotch-Irish blood.[¶]

The versatile Sir Francis Hincks is said to have been of the same blood.[**]

---

* The Scotch-Irish in America, Fourth Congress, p. 178.

† Dr. D. Hayes Agnew, by Dr. J. Howe Adams, Fifth Scotch-Irish Congress, p. 202.

‡ "Both the father and mother of Joseph Henry came from the southwest of Scotland, where the old family name was Hendrie. * * * the traditions of the family on both sides and the lion on the coat of arms point back to Irish ancestry of the highest rank; * * * he had a Scotch-Irish wife."—Professor G. Macloskie in "Joseph Henry" in The Scotch-Irish in America, Fifth Congress, p. 100.

§ The mother of Thomas A. Edison, who was Miss Elliott, is of Scotch-Irish blood, says Dr. Bryson.—The Scotch-Irish in America, Fourth Congress, p. 188.

¶ The Scotch-Irish in Canada by Stuart Acheson, in The Scotch-Irish in America, Third Congress, pp. 203 and 204. Dr. William Warren Baldwin, the father of Robert Baldwin, took the degree of M.D. at Edinburgh. He came to this country from a place near Cork, Ireland. Robert Baldwin was born in Toronto in 1804.—*Cyclopædia of Canadian Biography* by George McLean Rose.

** The Scotch-Irish in Canada by S. Acheson, just referred to, p. 206. Sir Francis Hincks was born in Cork, Ireland, son of Thomas Dix Hincks, a Presbyterian minister. The latter was born in Dublin and married Anne Boult of Chester. He was a son of Edward Hincks (m. Dix) who moved from Chester.—See *Dictionary of National Biography*, Appleton's

It is interesting to know that our associate James Bryce, the sympathetic and painstaking writer of the *American Commonwealth*, is a grandson of a Presbyterian minister of the north of Ireland and a Scotch-Irishman.*

The Scotch-Irish emigrants to this country were, generally speaking, men of splendid bodies and perfect digestion. They were men, too, of marked mental characteristics, which have impressed themselves on their posterity. They were plain, industrious and frugal in their lives. It has been said, such was their thrift, that Poor Richard himself could have given them "no new lessons against wastefulness and prodigality."†

But they had good intellectual powers and strong wills. They were notable for practical sagacity and common sense, and for tenacity of purpose. Conscious of their merits they were self-reliant and always ready to assert themselves, to defend their own rights and those of their neighbors, and courageously push forward. Plain in speech, they were not infrequently frank to the point of rudeness. With energy and firmness, while often hard, they were affectionate towards persons who conciliated them, hospitable and

---

Cyclopædia of American Biography and *Cyclopæaedia of Canadian Biography* just mentioned.

* Rev. James Bryce (1767–1857) went from Scotland, where he was born, to Ireland, and settled in 1805, as minister of the anti-burgher church in Killaig, Co. Londonderry. His son, James Bryce (1806–1877), was born in Killaig (near Coleraine). In 1846, appointed to the High School, Glasgow. See *Dictionary of National Biography*, to which the information contained in the article on the Bryces was furnished by the family. James Bryce, the writer of the *American Commonwealth*, the son and grandson of the persons just mentioned, was born in Belfast, Ireland, May 10th, 1838. His mother was (or is) Margaret, eldest daughter of James Young, Esquire, of Abbeyville, Co. Antrim.—See *Men and Women of the Time*, Thirteenth edition, 1891.

† Governor Bell in "Londonderry Celebration," etc., pp. 23, 24.

faithful. Their sedateness was qualified by their wit and humor.

The Scotch-Irish were led to come to this country, not only by the desire to better their material condition and to escape persecution, but by a spirit of daring.

As we have seen they took up their abode on our frontiers and defended us from the depredations of Indians, and did a large portion of the fighting required in our wars. They were ardent promoters of civil and religious liberty. As was to be expected, these Scotch Calvinists breathed the spirit of John Knox and contended fervently that the final regulation of political action belongs to the people.

For many years, also, they had been fighting for religious liberty in Scotland and Ireland, and, taught by ecclesiastical and governmental oppression, had become the warmest adherents of religious liberty. The Scotch-Irish were a devout and religious people, and constant and earnest Bible readers. In many a home in this land they reproduced the beautiful picture of domestic piety which has been painted by the genius of the immortal Scottish poet, Burns, in the Cotter's Saturday Night.

The Scotch-Irish, however, were never content with a sentimental piety, but sought always with tremendous earnestness, to place religion on a basis of knowledge and thought. They were men, too, of high moral principle and marked integrity. Another characteristic which never failed to appear among settlements of this people, was a mighty zeal for education. They were never content with the lower grades of common schools, but demanded, everywhere, classical high schools, and later, colleges and universities. Look at the schools which they established in Londonderry* and other New Hampshire towns. In the little town of Cherry Valley, in New York, they opened the first classical school in the

---

* Parker, pp. 82, 83, 119 et seq., 128.—Bell in "Londonderry Celebration," etc., p. 32.

central and western portions of that great State.* They seem to have furnished the principal schoolmasters of all the provinces south of New York, prior to the Revolution, and it is noteworthy that a large portion of the leaders in that great movement in the lower Middle, and Southern States, received their education under men of this race.† From them they undoubtedly caught an ardent love of liberty and an increased glow of patriotism.

Religion, virtue, and knowledge were three passions of the Scotch-Irish. With them piety was never divorced from education, and religion, as stated before, was based upon an intellectual foundation and what they believed to be a basis of knowledge.

I began this paper by saying that the Puritan owed a tribute to the Scotch-Irishman. There is much in common between them, but I have not time to dwell upon the resemblances in their characters and careers. They agreed in their views of religious truth and duty, and in their zeal and firmness in resisting civil and ecclesiastical domination. They were fellow sufferers for conscience' sake.

It has been claimed, and here I conclude, that the Scotch-Irish in this country while eager to enjoy religious liberty for themselves, have been ready to grant it to others, and that in this respect they showed a better spirit than the Puritans.

Was not the difference caused by time, however?

The Scotch-Irish came here a hundred years later than the Puritans. Meanwhile the religious world had gone ahead and generally exercised a larger toleration.

---

* *Ibid.*, pp. 195, 196.
† What the Scotch-Irish have done for Education, by G. Macloskie, in Scotch-Irish in America, First Congress, pp. 90–101.—Campbell, Vol. II., p. 486, with the references to authorities cited.

BIBLIOGRAPHICAL NOTE

The Scotch-Irish in America. Proceedings of the Scotch-Irish Congress, at Columbia, Tenn., May 8–11,1889. Cincinnati: Robert Clark & Co., 1889.

—Proceedings and Addresses of the Second Congress, at Pittsburg, Pa., May 29 to June 1, 1890. Cincinnati: Robert Clarke & Co., 1890.

—Proceedings and Addresses of the Third Congress, at Louisville, Ky., May 14 to 17, 1891. Nashville, Tenn.: Publishing House of the Methodist Episcopal Church South; Barber & Smith, Agents.

—Proceedings and Addresses of the Fourth Congress, at Atlanta, Ga., April 28 to May 1, 1892. Nashville, Tenn.: Publishing House of the Methodist Episcopal Church South, Barber & Smith, Agents.

—Proceedings and Addresses of the Fifth Congress, at Springfield, Ohio, May 11 to 14, 1893. Nashville, Tenn.: Barber & Smith, Agents.

—Proceedings and Addresses of the Sixth Congress, at Des Moines, Iowa, June 7 to 10, 1894. Nashville, Tenn.: Barber & Smith, Agents.

These volumes of proceedings contain many papers of great value, and relate to the history of the Scotch-Irish race before coming to America and in this country.

In preparing the Report of the Council, I have made especial use of "The Scotch-Irish of the South," a paper in the first volume, by William Wirt Henry, and considerable use of "The Making of the Ulsterman," by J. S. Macintosh; "The Scotch-Irish of New England," by Arthur L. Perry, in the second volume; "The Scotch-Irish in Canada," by Stuart Acheson, in the third; "The Inventors of the Scotch-Irish race," by John H. Bryson, in the fourth; and "Our Naval Heroes," by D. C. Kelly, in the fifth volume.

Professor Arthur L. Perry's paper, read at the Second Congress, has been printed in pamphlet form. (Boston: printed by J. S. Cushing & Co.) As printed in the proceedings, portions of this paper were cut out and their places indicated by stars. These are given at length in the reprint.

Campbell, Douglas. "The Puritan in Holland, England and America." 2 v. New York: Harper & Brothers, 1892.

The matter regarding the Scotch-Irish is to be found in the last chapter of the second volume. That chapter, besides embodying much other material, gives a very good summary of a large portion of the information brought out in the first three Congresses of the Scotch-Irish, correcting in some cases statements made in papers read in those meetings. I have been much indebted to Mr. Campbell's chapter, but think that it needs careful revision.

For a history of the Scotch-Irish before coming to America, see —

Froude, James Anthony. "The English in Ireland in the Eighteenth Century." 3 v. London, 1874.

Lecky, W. E. H. "A History of England in the Eighteenth Century." 8 v. New York, 1878–1890. London, 1878–1890.

Harrison, John. "The Scot in Ulster." Edinburgh and London, 1888.

The work of Mr. Harrison is a little volume which contains a valuable epitome of the history of the Scotch-Irish in Ulster, from the beginning of the Seventeenth Century to the present time. It is founded upon the best authorities, which appear to have been carefully consulted. I have made free use of Mr. Harrison's statements in preparing the earlier portions of my paper.

The more important works referred to by Mr. Harrison are the following:—

Calendar of State Papers. Ireland, 1603.

Register of the Privy Council of Scotland, vol. 8.

The Montgomery Manuscripts. Belfast, 1869.

The Hamilton Manuscripts. Belfast, 1867.

State Papers of James VI. (Abbottsford Club.)

Extracts from the Records of the Burgh of Glasgow, vols. 1630 to 1662.

Rushworth, John. Historical Collections, 1618 to 1648.

Fraser's Magazine, for article on Ulster and its people. July-Dec., 1876.

Reid, James. History of the Presbyterian Church in Ireland.

Thomson's Acts of Scottish Parliament.

Benn, George. History of Belfast.

Knox, Alexander. History of the County of Down. Dublin, 1875.

Hill, George. The Macdonnels of Antrim.

Hill, George. The Plantation in Ulster.

Gardiner's Fall of the Monarchy of Charles I., chaps. 15 and 16.

Balfour's Annals of Scotland.

Memorials of the troubles in Scotland. (Spalding Club.)

Turner, Sir James. Memoirs of his own life and time.

Prendergast's Cromwellian Settlement of Ireland.

Woodrow's History of the Sufferings of the Church of Scotland.

Petty, Sir William. Political Survey of Ireland. London, 1719.

Leland's History of Ireland.

Macpherson's History of Commerce.

Macaulay's History of England, Chapter 12 (Defence of Londonderry).

Walker's True account of the Siege of Londonderry. London, 1689.

Articles in the Ulster Journal of Archaeology.

Young, Arthur. A Tour in Ireland, made in the years 1776–'77–'78.

Other works on this period of Scotch-Irish history which may be examined with advantage are —

Plowden, Francis. Historical Review of the state of Ireland. Phila., 1805–6. 5 v. 8°.

Futhey, J. Smith. Historical discourse delivered on the 150th anniversary of the Octorara church, Chester Co., Pa.

> Long extracts from this address are given in Smith's "History of Peterborough," to be found later on in this list.

In regard to the history of the Scotch-Irish in New England, besides the paper of Professor Perry, it is desirable to refer to the following works:—

MAINE.—Willis, William. The Scotch-Irish immigration to Maine, and Presbyterianism in New England (Article I. in Collections of the Maine Historical Society, Vol. VI., Portland).

NEW HAMPSHIRE.—State Papers of New Hampshire,—particularly "Towns," Vol. 14, and "Muster Rolls," Vol. 2.

—Parker, Edward L. The History of Londonderry, comprising the towns of Derry and Londonderry, N. H. Boston: Perkins & Whipple, 1851.

> I have made large use of the history of Parker and the paper of Willis in preparing this paper.

—Smith, Albert. History of the town of Peterborough, Hillsborough County, New Hampshire, etc. Boston: Press of George H. Ellis, 1876.

—Morrison, Leonard A. The History of Windham, N. H. Boston: Cupples, Upham & Co., 1883.

—Belknap, Jeremy. History of New Hampshire.

—The Londonderry Celebration, Exercises on the 150th anniversary of the settlement of Old Nutfield, June 10, 1809.

Compiled by Robert C. Mack. Manchester: Published by John B. Clarke, 1870.

—Stark, Caleb. Memoir and official correspondence of General J. Stark, etc. Concord,1860.

—Addresses at the dedication of the monument erected to the memory of Matthew Thornton, at Merrimack, N. H., September 29, 1892. Published by authority of the State. Concord, N. H. The Republican Press Association, 1894.

VERMONT.—Thompson, Zadoc. History of Vermont, national, civil and statistical, in three parts.

Look in the Gazetteer of Vermont, which is part three of this work, under such headings as "Londonderry," "Landgrove," etc.

—McKeen's History of Bradford, Vermont.

MASSACHUSETTS. *Worcester.*—Records of the Proprietors of Worcester, Massachusetts. Edited by Franklin P. Rice. In Collections of the Worcester Society of Antiquity, Vol. III. Worcester, Mass.: Published by the Society, 1881.

—Early records of the town of Worcester, 1722–1821. In Collections of the Worcester Society of Antiquity, Vols. 2, 4, 8, 10, Part 1 of 11.

The Worcester Society of Antiquity will continue the publication of the records of the town.

—Deeds at Registry of Deeds.

Worcester County was formed July 10, 1731. Deeds recorded before that date can be consulted at the Registry of Deeds in Middlesex County, at Cambridge, as Worcester belonged to Middlesex County before Worcester County was formed.

—The records of births and deaths in Worcester.

—Worcester births, marriages and deaths. Compiled by Franklin P. Rice. Part I—Births. Worcester, Mass.: The Worcester Society of Antiquity, 1894. In Collections of the Worcester

Society of Antiquity, Vol. XII., Worcester, Mass.: Published by the Society, 1894.

—Inscriptions from the old Burial Grounds in Worcester, Massachusetts, from 1727 to 1859, with biographical and historical notes. In Collections of the Worcester Society of Antiquity, Vol. I.

—Lincoln, William. History of Worcester. Worcester: Moses D. Phillips & Co., 1837.

—with additions by Charles Hersey, 18G2.

—Wall, Caleb A. Reminiscences of Worcester. Worcester, Mass.: Printed by Tyler & Seagrave, 1877.

—Holland, Josiah Gilbert. History of Western Massachusetts, 2 v. Springfield: Published by Samuel Bowles & Co., 1855.

—Waldo Family.—New England Historical and Genealogical Register, XVIII., 176,177.

—Bridgman, Thomas. Inscriptions on monuments in King's Chapel Burial Ground. Boston, 1853. pp. 292, 293.

—Family Memorials by Edward E. Salisbury (p. 21) 1885. Privately printed.

—The Scotch-Irish in New England (George H. Smyth). In The Magazine of American History, vol. 9, p. 153.

—Scotch-Irish in New England (W. Willis). In New England Historical and Genealogical Register, 12; 231.

CANADA.—Miller, Thomas. Historical and genealogical record of the first settlers of Colchester County down to the present time. Halifax, Nova Scotia: A. & W. MacKinlay, 1873.

—Patterson, George. A History of the County of Pictou, Nova Scotia. Montreal: Dawson Brothers, 1877.

Proud, Robert. History of Pennsylvania, 1681–1742. Philadelphia: 1797–98. 2 V. 8°.

Scotch-Irish in Pennsylvania. In New England Historical and Genealogical Register, 16; 360.

Ramsay, David. History of South Carolina, 1670–1808.

Charleston, 1809. 2 v. 8°.

—History of the American Revolution. Philadelphia, 1789. 2 v. 8°.

—History of the Revolution in South Carolina. Trenton, 1785. 2 v. 8°.

Baird, Robert. Religion in the United States of America. Glasgow and London, 1844.

Craighead, J. G. Scotch and Irish Seeds in American Soil. Philadelphia: Presbyterian Board of Publication, 1878.

Scotch-Irish (J. C. Linehan). In Granite Monthly, vol. 11.

Scotch-Irish. Granite Monthly, vol. 12.

Scotch-Irish in America (G. H. Smyth). In Magazine of American History, 4; 161.

McCulloch, Hugh. Men and measures of half a century. Charles Scribner's Sons, 1888.

Appleton's Cyclopædia of American Biography, under the words "Matthew Thornton," "Asa Gray," etc.

APPENDIX

Letters which followed the appearance of brief reports of the contents of the foregoing paper in Boston newspapers.

The *Boston Traveller*, May 1, 1895.
SCOTCH-IRISH IN AMERICA.
Thomas Hamilton Murray criticises Samuel Swett Green's Essay upon this subject.

To the Editor:

Lawrence, April 26.—I have just read a synopsis of the essay by Samuel Swett Green, A.M., on the Scotch-Irish, so called, in America.

The essay was delivered on April 24, at a meeting in Boston of the American Antiquarian Society.

While I have the greatest respect, personally, for Mr. Green, I am obliged to impugn his reliability as an historian when he treats of the "Scotch-Irish" shibboleth. I must also take issue with him both as regards his premises and conclusions in the essay just mentioned. I do this because both are fatally defective and based on radically false assumptions. Mr. Green, beyond all question, intended to be accurate and honest in his paper before the Antiquarian Society. His sources of information, however, were misleading and unfortunate.

If I may take his paper as a criterion, he is not very well posted on Irish history—ancient, mediæval or modern. Neither, taking the same paper as a basis, does he appear to be well informed on the component elements of the Irish people. Lacking the essential basic knowledge, therefore, he has made a hodge-podge of the subject treated in endeavoring to prove too much.

This idea also seems to have struck Dr. Hale at the meeting in question, who wondered if Mr. Green claimed Columbus as

Scotch-Irish. The absurdity of some of the speaker's claims was also noted at the meeting by that excellent historian, Prof. Jameson of Brown University.

Mr. Green, like most people who use the mistaken term "Scotch-Irish," appears to do so under the supposition that it is synonymous with Protestant-Irish. Not so. Thousands of Protestant-Irish are of English descent, with not a drop of Scotch blood in their veins. Other thousands are of Huguenot extraction, a point with which Mr. Green does not appear to have been acquainted. Welsh, German and Dutch blood also enters materially into this Protestant-Irish element.

The number of Protestant-Irish of English descent who came to the colonies, when compared with Protestant-Irish of possible Scotch descent, was as 8 to 1, while the number of Keltic or Catholic Irish who came at the same period was as 20 to 1. Yet, Mr. Green seems never to have heard of either the Anglo-Irish or the Catholic Irish in the upbuilding of New England.

The Irish immigrants to this country who were actually of Scottish ancestry were at that time called, and were content to be called, merely Irish. It remained for a later generation of "historians," unable to suppress or deny the nationality of these comers, to dub them with what was intended to be a palliating term, Scotch-Irish.

Mr. Green makes another blunder in regarding all Ulstermen as of Scotch descent. With him the fact that a man hailed from the northern province is sufficient to stamp him as "Scotch-Irish." To any student of Irish history the fallacy of this is at once evident. Why, some of the most ancient blood in Ireland comes from Ulster, and at the time of the English conquest thousands of Catholic Ulstermen were exiled and settled all along the New England coast, from Maine to Connecticut. These Mr. Green would no doubt calmly appropriate as "Scotch-Irish."

His assertion that the Sullivans, John and James, were of Scotch extraction is so utterly nonsensical as not to merit a serious reply.

His claim that the Perrys were "Scotch-Irishmen" will make Rhode Islanders laugh. The mother of the Perrys was content to be known as a plain, everyday Irish woman. She was a daughter of an Irish rebel, and was never guilty of using a "Scotch" or any other extenuating prefix.

Mr. Green would have us understand that emigration from Scotland to Ireland commenced at the beginning of the 17th century. In this he is over a thousand years out of the way. Migration and emigration between the two countries began many centuries earlier than the 17th, or when Scotland became an Irish colony. When that was Mr. Green can easily ascertain by giving the matter proper attention and careful inquiry.

Alluding to the Presbyterian Irish who settled at Worcester, Mr. Green again rings the changes on the "Scotch-Irish," and says they introduced the Irish potato. But to be consistent, why does he not call it the Scotch-Irish potato? Why let the Irish-Irish have the credit?

In very truth this "Scotch-Irish" fad has become an unutterable bore. While some Irish people of immediate or remote Scottish descent did unquestionably come to these shores, not five per cent. of those claimed as such by current writers were really of Scotch extraction. And these were so hopelessly overwhelmed in numbers by other Irish who came, that any attempt to claim exclusive merit for the handful, can only result in mortification to the claimant.

The Protestant John Mitchell declares that "Scotch-Irish is a cant term coined by bigots." He then goes on to state that in Ireland the term was seldom or never heard.

A friend of mine, an Episcopalian, once said: "I notice that so long as an Irishman goes to the Roman Catholic Church he is spoken of as Irish; but should he change his creed and frequent the Baptist or the Methodist Church he is immediately referred to by his new friends as 'Scotch-Irish.'" This is a fair specimen of the shaky ground on which the shibboleth rests.

Most Rev. Dr. Plunkett, Protestant archbishop of Dublin, speaking on the "Scotch" and other prefixes, eloquently disapproves the same and warmly declares: "In truth, we are simply Irish, and nothing else."

THOMAS HAMILTON MURRAY.

This letter also appeared in *The Pilot*, Boston, in the issue of May 11. Following is a reply which was printed in *The Pilot* of June 15.

The same letter, substantially, had appeared in the *Boston Traveller* of May 3, in answer to Mr. Murray's letter of May 1.

THE "SCOTCH-IRISH" AGAIN.

Editor of *The Pilot:*

WORCESTER, MASS., May 11, 1895.—A marked copy of *The Pilot* of to-day has been sent to me, calling my attention to a communication from Thomas Hamilton Murray, in which Mr. Murray criticises statements which he supposes me to have made in a paper which I read before the American Antiquarian Society recently, and opinions which he supposes me to hold. He is laboring under misapprehensions as to my views.

Will you kindly allow me to correct some of these mistakes? They arise mainly from the fact that Mr. Murray did not hear the paper read and has not had an opportunity to read it himself.

He writes:—"Thousands of Protestant-Irish are of English descent, with not a drop of Scotch blood in their veins. Other thousands are of Huguenot extraction, a point with which Mr. Green does not appear to have been acquainted."

In my paper I stated that William III. exerted himself to bring colonies of Huguenots to the North of Ireland after the revocation of the Edict of Nantes. I mentioned also English colonists. I stated, too, that the Irish who were of Scotch blood intermarried with those of English-Puritan and Huguenot blood in Ireland.

My subject, however, was the Irish of Scotch blood.

Mr. Murray says: "Mr. Green seems never to have heard of either the Anglo-Irish or the Catholic-Irish in the upbuilding of New England." I am perfectly aware that both of these classes of Irishmen have had great influence here, but, as stated before, I limited myself in the paper to the influence of the Irish of Scotch descent.

Mr. Murray says: "The Irish immigrants to this country who were actually of Scottish ancestry were at that time called, and were content to be called, merely Irish."

I have not supposed that the Irish of Scottish blood were content to be called "merely Irish." See, for example, the letter of Rev. James McGregor, of Londonderry, N. H., to Governor Shute of Massachusetts, as quoted by Jeremy Belknap, by Parker in his *History of Londonderry*, N. H. (p. 68), and Lincoln in his *History of Worcester*, Mass. (p. 49.)

"Mr. Green makes another blunder," writes Mr. Murray, "in regarding all Ulster-men as of Scotch descent."

I hold no such belief, but chose to single out the inhabitants of Ulster of Scotch descent.

By reading a note appended to the names of General John Sullivan and Governor James Sullivan in my paper, Mr. Murray would see that I agree with him in finding no reasons for believing that they had Scotch blood. Am I wrong in believing that Miss Sarah Alexander, of Newry, Ireland, who married the father of Oliver Hazard Perry, was the granddaughter of James Wallace, an officer of the Scotch army and a signer of the Solemn League and Covenant, and that he fled in 1660 from County Ayr to the North of Ireland? If I am, I should be grateful to Mr. Murray if he would correct me.

Mr. Murray says, "Mr. Green would have us understand that emigration from Scotland to Ireland commenced at the beginning of the seventeenth century." I would not have anybody so understand, but, as I stated at the beginning of my paper, I selected for treatment the emigration during that century.

My old friend, Rev. Dr. Hale, expressed himself as much pleased with my paper, and would be very much surprised to learn that he was understood as disputing statements made by me because a jocose remark occurred to him.

Professor Jameson, whom, with Mr. Murray, I regard as an "excellent historian," took particular pains to say, at the meeting where my paper was read, that he had no objections to make to any statements which I had made, but had some doubt about the Scotch descent of one or more of the persons mentioned in a quotation which I had made from the history of Douglas Campbell.

Remarks about the "Irish potato" were made by me in a letter which I sent to you a week ago, and it is unnecessary for me to repeat here what you already have in that letter.

In regard to my sources of information, which Mr. Murray thinks were "misleading," I refer him to a somewhat long list of authorities given at the close of my paper.

I do not imagine that Mr. Murray and I could agree entirely, but I am sure that we agree more nearly than he has supposed, and that such an approach to agreement would appear if he were to read my paper. I hope that it will be printe * in a few months; and when it is printed, he can learn, if he wishes, exactly what I have written.

SAMUEL SWETT GREEN.

The letter in which there were remarks about the Irish potato was called out by the following paragraph in *The Pilot* of May 4:

There is something appropriate in the claim made by Dr. S. S. Green, of Worcester, before the American Antiquarian Society of Boston, on April 24, that the "Irish potato" was introduced into Worcester, as well as into many other places in America, by the "Scotch-Irish." It was just like the enterprising Scotch-Irishman to do that. He is the only creature in the whole wide realm of fiction who would have thought of "introducing" a vegetable to the land of its birth. Somebody with time on his hands and a laudable ambition to dispense the information, should tell the American Antiquarian Society that the potato is indigenous to America, and that the name "Irish potato" is as much a sham and a misnomer as the other name, "Scotch Irish," with this difference, that the vegetable is a real potato of American origin, while the human hybrid is neither Scotch nor Irish.

Following is the letter, with comments as it appeared in *The Pilot* of May 18.

THE "IRISH" POTATO.

Editor of *The Pilot:*

Worcester, Mass., May 4, 1895.—Will you kindly allow me to correct a mistake which was made by the writer of a paragraph in to-day's issue of your paper, regarding a statement recently made by me in an essay read before the American Antiquarian Society in Boston.

The writer does not understand how the potato could have been introduced into Worcester and other places in this neighborhood during the eighteenth century when it is indigenous to America.

There is no doubt that it is indigenous on this continent and no doubt that it was carried from this country to Europe in the sixteenth century. It is also true, however, that it was introduced into Worcester and other places in this country in the eighteenth century by emigrants from the North of Ireland.

About 200 persons, who were a portion of a party of three or four times that number which arrived in Boston, August 4, 1718, went to Worcester, and were among its earlier settlers.

Most of this body of emigrants from the North of Ireland were of Scotch extraction, as is well known. A few of them, however, were of pure Irish blood. Of the latter was a family of Youngs who went to Worcester. They are credited with the introduction of the potato there. The people of Worcester knew little or nothing about that vegetable before. Their ignorance is shown by an anecdote which has come down to us and which is narrated in Lincoln's *History of Worcester*.

After writing that "it is remarkable that the esculent, now considered essentially necessary for table and farm should have been introduced at a period so late," Lincoln continues: "It is related, that some of our early inhabitants, after enjoying the hospitality of one of the Irish families, were each presented with a few potatoes for planting. Unwilling to give offence by refusing the present, they accepted the donation; but suspecting the poisonous quality, they carried the roots only to the next swamp, and there threw them away, as unsafe to enter their homes." (p. 49, note 2.)

Speaking of the portion of the emigrants from the North of Ireland who came over in 1718 and, with others of their countrymen who soon joined them, settled at Londonderry, N. H., Parker, the historian of that town, writes: "They introduced the culture of the potato, which they brought with them from Ireland. Until their arrival, this reliable vegetable, now regarded as one of the necessaries of life, if not wholly unknown, was not cultivated in New England. To them belongs the credit of its introduction to general use. Although highly prized by this company of settlers, it was for a long time but little regarded by their English neighbors, a barrel or two being considered a supply for a family. But its value as food for man and for beast became at length more generally known, and who can now estimate the full advantage of its cultivation to this country! The following well-authenticated fact will show how little known to the community at large the potato must have been.

A few of the settlers had passed the winter previous to their establishment here, in Andover, Mass. On taking their departure from one of the families, with whom they had resided, they left a few potatoes for seed. The potatoes were accordingly planted; some came up and flourished well; blossomed and produced balls, which the family supposed were the fruit to be eaten. They cooked the balls in various ways, but could not make them palatable, and pronounced them unfit for food. The next spring, while ploughing their garden, the plough passed through where the potatoes had grown, and turned out some of great size, by which means they discovered their mistake." (pp. 48 and 49.)

It appears natural after this statement of facts that the potato should have been very generally called the Irish potato, in Worcester and elsewhere.

I remember perfectly that in my boyhood, fifty years ago, and afterwards when we had two kinds of potatoes on the table, in my father's family, we were always asked whether we would have a sweet potato or an Irish potato. The name is still used to a considerable extent.

Truly yours,
'Samuel Swett Green.'

[We make room, with pleasure, for Mr. Green's letter. It was only in the interest of historical accuracy that we deprecated the use of the term "Irish potato," as that esculent is a peculiarly American product; and, as Mr. Green avows, it certainly is not a "Scotch-Irish" vegetable. The introduction of the American potato into Ireland was, unhappily, a Nessus-gift. The fatal facility of its culture led the people to place unwise dependence upon it; so that when the "blight" of 1847 came, they found themselves without other means of existence, and, as a consequence, 1,225,000 human beings died of the "Great Famine" of that year. It was a sad day for Ireland when it first knew the potato; but if America has profited by its repatriation, give the credit to Irish, not Scotch, Ireland.—*Editor Pilot.*

Mr. Murray continued the correspondence by sending the

following letter to the Worcester *Telegram*, June 27, 1895.

To the Editor of *The Telegram:*

Samuel Swett Green, A. M., of Worcester, a short time ago read a paper in Boston before the American Antiquarian Society. His subject was the Scotch-Irish, so-called, among our early immigrants.

I took exceptions to many statements by Mr. Green as they were reported in the Boston journals at the time, several days having elapsed between the appearance of said reports and the publication of my criticism.

As Mr. Green had not questioned the general accuracy of these newspaper reviews of his essay, I was entirely justified in making them the basis of my objections. And this the more so, from the fact that the different papers—the *Globe, Journal* and others—practically agreed in their statement of the salient points.

Since then Mr. Green has replied, both in the *Boston Traveller* and the *Boston Pilot*, to the adverse criticism I had advanced. I wish to acknowledge at the outset the courteous language of his reply, and his frank, honest method of discussing the subject with me. It is a pleasure to have a disputant of Mr. Green's ability, character and good nature. His calm, judicial mind is not impervious to argument, nor does he close his ears, because he may, perhaps, hear something that runs counter to previously conceived ideas.

Mr. Green says: "I do not imagine that Mr. Murray and I could agree entirely, but I am sure that we agree more nearly than he has supposed, and that such an approach to agreement would appear if he were to read my paper."

I am glad Mr. Green displays this conciliatory spirit of arbitration, for it goes a great way toward a satisfactory discussion of the subject.

In answer to my criticisms he makes several important admissions, viz.: (1) People from the north of Ireland are not necessarily of Scotch descent. (2) Thousands of north of Ireland Protestants and thousands of Protestants from other parts of Ireland have come to this country who were not of Scottish ancestry. (3) The term Scotch-Irish is not equivalent to that of Protestant-Irish. (4) The Catholic Irish have had great influence here, before, during and since the revolution. (5) The Sullivans, John and James, were not of Scottish ancestry. Several other admissions are likewise made by Mr. Green, all of which bring us nearer together in point of general agreement.

Mr. Green says in explanation of his paper that he limited himself to "the Irish of Scotch descent."

Ah! that is better. So long as he strictly adheres to it—not claiming as of Scotch descent Irishmen who are not—just so long will he have no contention. Rather do I praise him for his efforts in that respect.

Any writer who honestly aims to give any section of Irish settlers in this country a deserved meed of praise shall always have my respect and encouragement. It is only when Irish are claimed as of Scotch descent, who are not, or when exclusive merit is claimed for those who are, I object. In this respect I think that Mr. Green will frankly admit that my position is an entirely proper one.

No man of sense can properly object to the term "Irish of Scotch descent," when rightly used, whereas the term "Scotch-Irish" is open to very grave objections from many points of view. Mr. Green will, I think, recognize the point.

We of the old Irish race draw no invidious distinctions, but receive into brotherhood all born on Irish soil, or of Irish parents, regardless of creed and no matter where their grandfather or great-grandfather may have come from.

It is a fact, as no doubt Mr. Green is aware, that thousands of north of Ireland Catholics are of Scottish descent on one side or the other. It is also true that many of the best friends of Irish nationality, autonomy and independence have been of the same element, Protestant and Catholic. But they were simply "Irish," look you. They weighted down their birthright with no extenuating prefix or palliating affix.

It is a blunder to suppose that all the Irish settlers in New Hampshire were of "Scottish descent." Many of the most prominent who located there were not. Yet because some were, hasty writers have jumped to the conclusion that all were of Scotch ancestry. A more lamentable error it would be difficult to fall into.

I stated in my first reply to Mr. Green that the early Irish immigrants to this country who were actually (and not by recent pretence) of Scottish ancestry were content to be called merely Irish. Mr. Green appears unwilling to admit this and quotes a letter of Rev. James McGregor, of Londonderry, N. H., to Gov. Shute, of Massachusetts. But while McGregor may have been unwilling to acknowledge himself or his immediate associates as pure, unalloyed Irish, there is no real evidence that the bulk of New Hampshire's Irish settlers agreed with him. Lincoln, the Worcester historian, no matter how excellently informed in other respects, cannot, to my mind, be recognized as an authority on early Irish immigration. And this comment must also apply to Dr. Hale and Prof. Jameson—both of whom are admirably posted on other phases of New England history, but lamentably deficient in this.

Against McGregor, above mentioned, I place McSparran. Parson McSparran, I need not tell Mr. Green, was an Irish Protestant clergyman who for nearly forty years (from 1721) was rector of St. Paul's Church in Narragansett. Although of Scottish ancestry and partly educated in Scotland, he never spoke of himself as "Scotch-Irish." Yet if the term were ever justifiable, it would have been so in his case. The expression "Scotch-Irish" never occurs in McSparran's writings. He always alludes to himself as "Irish," as being an "Irishman," and as able to speak, read and write "the Irish language." He was proud of his Irish nationality, and while not loving the land of his ancestors less, admired that of his nativity more.

McSparran in his quaint work, American Dissected, thus speaks of early New Hampshire settlers:

"In this province lies that town called London-Derry, all Irish, and famed for industry and riches."

Leaving New Hampshire, he continues:

"Next you enter Main (e), which, in its civil government, is annexed to the Massachusetts, as Sagadahock also is, and both rather by use than right. In these two eastern provinces many Irish are settled, and many have been ruined by the French Indians."

No mention of "Scotch-Irish," you will notice! Yet McSparran was in close touch with his countrymen throughout New England. Again he writes:

"It is pretty true to observe of the Irish, that those who come here with any wealth are the worse for their removal, though doubtless the next generation will not suffer so much as their fathers; but those who, when they came, had nothing to lose, have throve greatly by their labors."

Again, referring to Pennsylvania, he says: "By the accessions of the Irish and Germans, they threaten, in a few years, to lessen the American demands for Irish and other European linens."

Speaking of Maryland, McSparran declares "There are some Quakers here * * * and some Irish Presbyterians, owing to the swarms that, for many years past, have winged their way westward out of the great Hibernian hive."

Referring to Pennsylvania, he writes: "The Irish are numerous in this province, who, besides their interspersions among the English and others, have peopled a whole county by themselves, called the county of Donegal, with many other new out-towns and districts."

McSparran gives absolutely no indication that he ever heard of the "Scotch-Irish" term. Certainly he never used it personally. His family, education and good sense placed him above such a cowardly subterfuge. A short time before his death he forwarded his diplomas of master and doctor to a cousin in Ireland, requesting that they be registered in the parish registry of Dungiven "so that my relatives in time to come might be able to speak of me with authority." Thus he marked for all time his identity as an Irishman.

The colonial records repeatedly mention the "Irish," not the Scotch-Irish. Cotton Mather in a sermon in 1700 says: "At length it was proposed that a colony of Irish might be sent over to check the growth of this countrey." No prefix there. The party of immigrants remaining at Falmouth, Me., over winter, and which later settled in Londonderry, N. H., were alluded to in the records of the general court as "poor Irish."

On St. Patrick's day, 1700, Irish of Portsmouth, N. H., instituted St. Patrick's lodge of Masons. Pretty good proof that they were content to be called merely "Irish." Later we find Stark's rangers at Fort Edward requesting an extra supply of grog so as to properly observe the anniversary of St. Patrick. Very little comfort here for your "Scotch-Irish" theorist.

Rev. John Moorhead, a Presbyterian minister of Boston, was born in the north of Ireland and received much of his education in Scotland. Yet he wished to be regarded as mere "Irish." In proof of this he joined the Charitable Irish Society of Boston in 1739, and made an address on that occasion. Only men of Irish birth or extraction could be admitted to actual membership in the society then as now. Mr. Moorhead in being thus admitted so acknowledged himself. His congregation is described by Drake, Condon, Cullen and other authorities, as being composed of "Irish Presbyterians."

No mention whatever is made of any "Scotch-Irish" in the neighborhood.

Marmion's maritime ports of Ireland states that "Irish families" settled Londonderry, N. H. Spencer declares that "the manufacture of linen was considerably increased by the coming of Irish immigrants." In 1723, says Condon, "a colony of Irish settled in Maine." Moore, in his sketch of Concord, N. H., pays tribute to the "Irish settlers" in that section of New England. McGee speaks of "the Irish settlement of Belfast," Me. The same author likewise declares that "Irish families also settled early at Palmer and Worcester, Mass." Cullen describes the arrival at Boston in 1717 of Capt. Robert Temple, "with a number of Irish Protestants." Capt. Temple was, in 1740, elected to the Charitable Irish Society. In another place Cullen alludes to "the Irish spinners and weavers who landed in Boston in the earlier part of the 18th century."

Many persons who continually sing the praises of the so-called "Scotch-Irish" stand in serious danger of being considered not only ignorant but positively dishonest. Their practice is to select any or all Irishmen who have attained eminence in American public life, lump them together and label the lump "Scotch-Irish."

Among those who have been thus wrongly claimed are Carroll, Sullivan, Knox, Moylan, Wayne, Barry, Clinton, Montgomery, Elliott, Hand and a host of others. Of a later period, Jackson, Calhoun, Meade and Sheridan have been ridiculously styled "Scotch-Irish." The late John Boyle O'Reilly has not yet been so styled, but no doubt will be after he has been dead long enough to make it comparatively safe.

Of the revolutionary heroes mentioned above, Charles Carroll was of old Irish stock. His cousin, John Carroll, was a Roman Catholic clergyman, a Jesuit, a patriot, a bishop and archbishop. Daniel Carroll was another sterling patriot.

The Sullivans, James and John, were also of ancient Irish stock, the name having been O'Sullivan even in their father's time.

Gen. Knox and his father were both members of the Charitable Irish Society of Boston. The general also belonged to the Friendly Sons of St. Patrick, Philadelphia.

Moylan was a brother of the Roman Catholic bishop of Cork.

Quickly would he have repudiated the term "Scotch-Irish."

Wayne was of Irish descent and proud of his Irish lineage. There is abundant evidence of this did space allow me to present it. He was an active member of the Friendly Sons of St. Patrick.

Barry was an Irish Roman Catholic. It was he who, when met by an English frigate on the high seas, replied to the commander's demand as to who he was, with "The United States ship Alliance, saucy Jack Barry, half Irishman, half Yankee—Who are you?"

The Clintons, George and James, were sons of a county Longford Irishman, who with a large family immigrated from Ireland in 1729.

Montgomery was an Irishman by birth and patriotism, and a native of county Donegal. His father was a member of the Irish parliament.

Brig.-Gen. Elliott was a member of the Charitable Irish Society of Boston, and at one time its president.

Hand was a native of Kings county, Ireland, and served in France with the Irish brigade. During our revolution he attained the rank of brigadier-general, and was a great favorite with Washington.

All the foregoing would have laughed had any attempt been made in their lifetime to tag them "Scotch-Irish."

Mr. Green asks: "Am I wrong in believing that Miss Sarah Alexander of Newry, Ireland, who married the father of Oliver Hazard Perry, was the grandaughter of James Wallace, an officer in the Scotch army and a signer of the Solemn League and Covenant, and that he fled in 1660 from county Ayr to the north of Ireland? If I am, should be gratified to Mr. Murray if he would correct me."

No general correction is necessary. Miss Alexander's grandfather, at least on the paternal side, was Scotch. But what of it? Sarah, his grandaughter, was an Irish woman—Irish by birth, education, sympathy and association. Would Mr. Green consider himself the less an American because his grandfather happened to be English or Irish or Scotch? Certainly not! He cannot, therefore, apply the law of nationality in his own case and refuse its application in that of Sarah Alexander. A man of his clear sense and logical mind will not, I am sure, after thinking it over, have any desire to do so.

Prejudiced or poorly informed writers have made sad work of this "Scotch-Irish" business. Thus Henry Cabot Lodge gives the absurd definition of "Scotch-Irish" as being "Protestant in religion and chiefly Scotch and English in blood." This has only been equalled in absurdity by Dr. McIntosh, who defined this elusive element as "not Scotch nor Irish, but rather British." Here we have two gentlemen claiming to speak as with authority, yet unable to agree even in first essentials. What an excellent farce, indeed, is all this.

Probably no man in recent years has done more to shatter the "Scotch-Irish" fallacy than Hon. John C. Linehan, the present state insurance commissioner of New Hampshire. His vast researches and able articles relative to the early settlers justly entitle him to be considered the historian of the Irish in the Granite state. His recent contributions on "How the Irish came as builders of the nation" contain a mass of priceless information regarding the Irish pioneers in Londonderry, Antrim, Dublin and other New Hampshire places.

Returning to the Charitable Irish Society, it should be stated that all the founders were Protestants—chiefly Presbyterians. Some of them were from the North of Ireland and may have had Scottish forefathers. But whether they had or not, all wished to be considered as simply "Irish." Had they desired to be considered "Scotch rather than Irish," they would have joined the Scotch Charitable Society—which was already inexistence in Boston. But no! They wanted a distinctively Irish organization, and consequently founded one on St. Patrick's day, 1737. You will particularly note that they named it the Charitable Irish Society and not the Charitable Scotch-Irish Society. Indeed, they make no use at any time of the latter hyphenated expression.

We admire the upright, sturdy Irishman; we have respect for the genuine Scotchman. But for the man who through ignorance or association is ashamed of his native land, and who represents himself as something he is not, we have only pity and contempt in about equal parts. The most sincere Orangeman I ever knew never dreamt of denying that he was an Irishman. With the mass of his countrymen he did not agree in religion or politics. But he knew, as they did, that these matters were separate, apart and distinct from his nativity or nationality.

But enough! Truth only is permanent. False assumptions, mistaken theories or deliberate misrepresentation may create for a time a certain impression. In the end, however, cold, stern, unrelenting fact will always prevail.

THOMAS HAMILTON MURRAY.

LAWRENCE, MASS., June 26, 1895.

The foregoing letter also appeared in the *Boston Herald* of June 28. The following reply was printed in the *Worcester Daily Telegram* of June 28. It was cut out from a copy of the *Telegram* and sent to the *Boston Herald*, but was not printed by that paper.

To the Editor of *The Telegram:*—

A very courteous letter appeared in this morning's *Telegram* from Thomas Hamilton Murray of Lawrence, in continuance of a correspondence regarding statements made by me in a paper read at the semi-annual meeting of the American Antiquarian Society, held in Boston the 24th of April last. Please allow me to say a few words in reply.

As no part of the correspondence has appeared in a Worcester paper, in so far as I know, I can best introduce the whole subject by asking you to print the following letter, which appeared in the *Boston Pilot*, June 15, in answer to a letter which was printed in the *Pilot* of May 11, and which had appeared before in the *Boston*

Traveller of May 1. A reply from me appeared in the *Traveller* May 3. The reply in the *Pilot*, although written May 11, was delayed in its appearance until June 15.

Here followed Mr. Green's first reply to Mr. Murray. The second letter went on as follows:

It appears from this letter that what Mr. Murray calls "admissions" were denials that I had made certain statements and held views which he supposed me to hold.[*] Mr. Murray gives reasons and extracts to show that the Irish of Scotch descent who came here in the 17th century were content to be called "merely Irish."

Now, I have no doubt that to a very considerable extent they associated with other Irishmen, and especially with Presbyterians from the North of Ireland, not of Scotch extraction, and I know that the name Irish was frequently applied to men of Scotch blood who had lived in Ireland. But there was strong feeling, too, between many of the Catholic and Protestant Irish, which began when the Scotch went to the North of Ireland in large numbers in the earlier parts of the 17th century and which was intensified by the troubles in 1688 between James II. and William III. There was a prejudice in this country, too, regarding the Irish.

It is believed in Worcester that one of the reasons why the settlers from the North of Ireland who came here in 1718 were cruelly treated, was that they were victims of that prejudice. Rev. Mr. McGregor's letter probably represented the views of many emigrants from the North of Ireland, on being termed "merely Irish."

Last May I received a letter from Hon. Leonard A. Morrison of Canobie Lake, N. H., in which he wrote: "I am one of Scotch-Irish blood, and my ancestors came with Rev. Mr. McGregor of Londonderry, and neither they nor any of their descendants were

---

[*] A misprint. I wrote "denials that I had made certain statements which he had supposed me to make and that I held views which he had supposed me to hold."

willing to be called 'merely Irish.' I have twice visited the parish of Aghedowary,* county Londonderry, from which they came in Ireland, and all that locality is filled, not with Irish, but with Scotch-Irish, and this is pure Scotch blood to-day, after more than 200 years. I can show you families here of as pure Scotch blood as you can find in the lowlands of Scotland, where there has never been a marriage with any but those of Scotch blood."

Mr. Morrison is the author of the History of Windham and several other books in which he has to deal largely with Irish of Scotch descent. I am not writing in a polemical spirit, but simply as a student of history, and it seems to me as such that a large portion of the emigrants from the North of Ireland in the 17th century were as proud of their Scottish descent as emigrants from Ireland of the last 50 years are proud of their Irish descent.

I do not understand why the late William Lincoln should not be trusted when he writes about the earlier settlers in Worcester from the North of Ireland. About 200 of the immigrants who reached Boston in August, 1718, from the North of Ireland came to Worcester. That number was as great probably as the population found here when they came. The new comers were, therefore, an important portion of the population of Worcester, whose history Mr. Lincoln wrote in such manner that his work holds a high place among town histories. He spoke of the colony of persons who came here in 1718 from the North of Ireland as "Scots." It seems to me that Jeremy Belknap, Rev. Mr. McGregor, and Messrs. Morrison and Lincoln may be trusted in regard to representations made by them respecting bodies of men among whose descendants they were living and about whom they had prepared themselves to write.

In regard to the use of the term Scotch-Irish, I did not realize that I should give offence by employing it, and I probably should have used some other designation to convey my meaning rather

---

* Misprint for Aghadowey.

than irritate bodies of men whom I respect. I used the word, however, only in a descriptive sense, just as I sometimes use the terms Afro-American and Swedish-American. I entirely agree with Mr. Murray that, generally speaking, it is best not to use words which show the differences of the inhabitants of a country rather than the things which they hold in common. For example, it is better to speak generally of Americans, rather than Irish-Americans or French-Americans.

Still men must make themselves understood in writing, and it is sometimes very convenient for purposes of description to place an adjective indicative of blood before the name denoting nationality. Thus, upon taking up a newspaper this morning, which recognizes in the highest degree the services of our fellow citizens of Irish blood, I found it speaking for descriptive purposes of "Irish-Americans."

Mr. Murray asks: "Would Mr. Green consider himself less an American because his grandfather happened to be English or Irish or Scotch?" "Certainly not,"* is his answer. Still if one of my grandfathers had been a Scotchman I do not think that I should be troubled, if I showed Scotch characteristics, should my acquaintances speak of me as a Scotch-American. It so happens that one of my grandmothers, Nancy Barber, was a descendant of one of the early settlers in Worcester of Scotch extraction. I have so little of her blood in my veins, however, that I suppose that nobody would think of calling me either an Irishman or Scotchman or Scotch-American. I think that I should preserve my equanimity were either of the three designations applied to me.

Mr. Murray speaks of the inconsistent definitions which are given by authors to the term Scotch-Irish. In so far as I am concerned, I

---

* I inserted the word "as" before "is." The omission in printing led Mr. Murray, it will be seen, to suppose that I had avoided a direct answer to a question which he asked.

gave my own definition on the first page of my paper, as follows: "The Scotch-Irish, as I understand the meaning of the term, are Scotchmen who emigrated to Ireland and such descendants of those emigrants as had not, through intermarriage with the Irish proper, or others, lost their Scotch characteristics. Both emigrants and their descendants, if they remained long in Ireland, experienced certain changes, apart from those which are brought about by mixture of blood, through the influence of new surroundings."

Mr. Murray speaks of the mistakes which have been made in ascribing Scotch blood to distinguished Irishmen. Of the persons named by him I have not claimed Scotch extraction for Carroll, Sullivan, Moylan, Wayne, Barry, Elliott, Hand, Meade or Sheridan. Nor do I expect to claim it for my friend, the late John Boyle O'Reilly, nor for my correspondent, and I think I may add, my friend, Mr. Murray, for either he or a predecessor on the Lawrence American has praised highly my methods of library management, still I must add that the Christian name "Hamilton" is a little suspicious. It has a Scotch look, and I am inclined to think that my friend may be related to Lord Dufferin, the descendant of the Nobleman Hamilton, who led a colony of Scotchmen into Ireland in James the first's time.

In regard to Knox, Clinton, Montgomery, Jackson and Calhoun, I must ask Mr. Murray to consider the testimony brought forward in the notes to my paper. Mr. Murray will be glad to hear that I have referred to some of Mr. Linehan's writings in the list of sources of information at the end of my paper.[*] I will try to add,

---

[*] Honorable John C. Linehan, Insurance Commissioner of the State of New Hampshire, has written several papers on the Scotch-Irish. He is of Irish blood and objects strenuously to the use of the term "Scotch-Irish." I wrote to him for a list of his writings in order that I might print it here. He could not give me one, but wrote that he expects to make a collection, in pamphlet form, of his papers on the general subject under consideration and have it printed the coming autumn (1895).

if not too late, Parson McSparran's work.*

I do not find it easy to reconcile Mr. Murray's statements regarding Rev. Dr. Hale and Prof. Jameson. In his letter in the *Traveller* and *Pilot*, in speaking of me as "lacking the essential basic knowledge" and so as having "made a hodge-podge of the subject treated in endeavoring to prove too much," he wrote: "This idea also seems to have struck Dr. Hale at the meeting in question. * * * The absurdity of some of the speaker's claims was also noted at the meeting by that excellent historian, Prof. Jameson of Brown University." In the letter in this morning's *Telegram* Mr. Murray, after saying that Lincoln cannot be "recognized as an authority on early Irish immigration," goes on to say: "And this comment must also apply to Dr. Hale and Prof. Jameson, both of whom are admirably posted on other phases of New England history, but lamentably deficient in this." Why the change in the estimate of these two men? Is it because they supported me in my views instead of opposing me?

Dr. Hale has wide interests and, I presume, knows much about Ireland and Scotland, and the Scotch who settled in Ireland. Prof. Jameson intimated at the meeting of the American Antiquarian Society at which my paper was read, that he was descended from an Irishman of Scotch extraction. He seemed, too, to be interested in the subject of my paper, and to have knowledge regarding it.

Yours truly,

SAMUEL SWETT GREEN.

Mr. Murray wrote again to the *Worcester Daily Telegram*. This letter was in the paper of July 8.

To the Editor of *The Telegram:*—

---

* For a reprint of *America Dissected*, by Rev. J. McSparran, D. D., see an appendix to *History of the Episcopal Church in Narragausett, Rhode Island*, by Wilkins Updike. New York, 1817.

Samuel Swett Green in your issue of the 28th ult., replies to my communication of a day or two previous anent the "Scotch-Irish," so called.

I take exceptions to certain points advanced by him in his latest contribution, as I have to others which he had previously brought forward.

Still, there is so much in his present reply in the nature of concession to my position, that our bone of contention is being rapidly reduced to a minimum. This is practically the outcome Mr. Green indicated would result as soon as we got together and compared views and notes. In his latest reply Mr. Green thus manfully writes:—

"In regard to the use of the term Scotch-Irish, I did not realize that I should give offence by employing it, and I probably should have used some other designation to convey my meaning rather than irritate bodies of men whom I respect. I used the word, however, only in a descriptive sense, just as I sometimes use the terms Afro-American and Swedish-American. I entirely agree with Mr. Murray that, generally speaking, it is best not to use words which show the differences of the inhabitants of a country rather than the things which they hold in common. For example, it is better to speak generally of Americans, rather than Irish-Americans or French-Americans."

After this candid admission very little remains to be said. So much of what I have been contending for is comprised in it that a vast amount of debris has been cleared away, thus enabling us to survey the field to better advantage.

The tendency nowadays among Americans of Irish extraction, is to drop the prefix Irish, and it is well that this is so. No more patriotic Americans can be found than those of immediate or remote Irish descent. And this has been so from the beginning. Ten years ago I wrote in the *Boston Globe* on the staff of which I was at the time, that it was in bad taste to insist on hampering an American on every possible occasion, with the prefix "Irish" or "German" or "French" or "Scotch." With as much or as little sense might the late Robert C. Winthrop be spoken of as an "English-American," or the Knickerbocker element in New York continue to be labelled "Dutch-Americans."

But the principle herein contained is not of recent conception. The bulk of the most progressive and highly educated people in Ireland of Scottish descent, have for centuries held like sentiments. In their own estimation they were "Irish" and wished to be so regarded. The evidence on this point is so overwhelmingly abundant that it seems a waste of time to dwell upon it. A few there were, no doubt, who were ashamed of their Irish nationality just as we have in our country to-day a certain class of wretched Anglo-maniacs who, despising their birthright, can admire nothing save what is English.

These patriotic Irish of Scotch descent, mentioned above, objected to being loaded down with a foreign prefix on the same principle that we Americans object to similar hyphenated terms. And they were right as we are right. What then must be thought of people to-day in this country who persistently label themselves Scotch-Irish or Scotch-Irish-Americans? Very little that is complimentary, I am sure.

Mr. Green quotes Hon. Leonard A. Morrison of Canobie Lake, N. H., who boasts that even after 200 years residence in Ireland his family still remained aliens. I pity the man who would make such a boast. At the same time, I can hardly suppress a smile at Mr. Morrison's breakneck anxiety to get away from the awful suspicion that he may be considered "merely Irish." But he is handicapped at the outset. His name—Morrison,—is deplorably Irish. In fact, few names can trace a longer pure Irish pedigree than his. The Morrison families, too, were proud ones among the old Irish nobility. The stem goes back to a period anterior even to the Irish colonization of Scotland. If Mr. Morrison wants pedigree and ancestral glory he will stick to Ireland. Still there is no accounting for tastes, and if he wishes to cut loose from the ancient Irish stock, we, who glory in that stock, will make no effort to detain him.

Hon. John C. Linehan, the historian of the Irish in New Hampshire, and now Insurance Commissioner of the State, thus writes:—

"In these latter days a new school of writers has sprung up, whose pride of ancestry outstrips their knowledge, and whose prejudices blind their love of truth. With the difference in religion between certain sections of the Irish people as a basis, they are bent in creating a new race, christening it 'Scotch-Irish,' laboring hard to prove that it is a 'brand' superior to either of the two old types, and while clinging to the Scotch root, claim that their ancestors were different from the Irish in blood, morals, language and religion. This is a question not difficult to settle for those who are disposed to treat it honestly, but, as a rule, the writers who are the most prolific, as well as the speakers who are the most eloquent, know the least about the subject, and care less, if they can only succeed in having their theories accepted. The Irish origin of the Scots is studiously avoided by nearly all the Scotch-Irish writers, or if mentioned at all, is spoken of in a manner which leaves the reader to infer that the Scots had made a mistake in selecting their ancestors, and it was the duty of their descendants, so far as it lay in their power, to rectify the error.

What a vast difference there is between the contracted spirit shown by Mr. Morrison, and the love for Ireland and the Irish which the great, big hearted Dr. McSparran displayed. What a difference, too, between Mr. Morrison, who tries to avoid kindred with the pure, unalloyed Irish, and Gen. John McNeil, another descendant of a Londonderry settler, who in 1830, joined the Charitable Irish Society, thus wishing to identify himself with the Sons of Hibernia.

In my previous letter to *The Telegram* alluding to Parson McSparran's work, the types made me say "Americans Dissected," it should be "America Dissected." Also when referring to St. Patrick's lodge of Masons, the date should have been 1770 and not 1700, as it appeared in print.

Commissioner Linehan says in speaking of the Irish arrivals in Worcester: "Rev. Edward Fitzgerald (a Scotch name in no sense whatever) was the first pastor of the Presbyterian church in Worcester, in 1718. His congregation had rather a sorry time of it trying to establish themselves in the Heart of the Commonwealth. The margin between the Congregational and Presbyterian churches was narrow, but the former widened it by tearing down the church of the newcomers, not leaving the timber, even, on the ground... John Young came to Worcester in 1718, from Ireland, with his family. The town historian, Lincoln, wrote that the 'Scotch-Irish' were accompanied by a few of the native Irish, and mentions Young as one of them; and that he was the first man to introduce the cultivation of the potato in Worcester. Here is a concession the mere Irish ought to be thankful for—that there were even a few came; but it certainly is queer that their Boston brethren persisted in calling themselves Irish, notwithstanding they were as Protestant as the Worcester or New Hampshire people of the same period."

Why anybody of Irish birth or descent should try to sink his glorious heritage and seek to establish himself as "Scotch rather than Irish," is something I cannot understand. Ireland possesses a far more ancient civilization than either Scotland or England. Her hagiology, her educational institutions, her old nobility, her code of laws, her jurisprudence, are of much greater antiquity. "The Irish," declares Collins, "colonized Scotland, gave to it a name, a literature and a language, gave it a hundred songs and gave it Christianity." For additional evidence on this point see Knight, Lingard, Chambers, Lecky, Venerable Bede, Buckle, Pinkerton,

Logan, Thebaud, Sir Henry Maine and other authors.

Mr. Joseph Smith, an Irish Protestant of Lowell, Mass., in a letter to the *Pilot* in September, 1892, alluding to a writer who dwells upon the "Scotch-Irish," says:—

"I object as an Irishman and a Protestant to having my race and religion misrepresented, and I most vigorously protest against a Scotchman's posing as the mouthpiece and defender of Irish Protestanism. The Irish Protestants need no defender; they have always been amply able to take care of themselves, and they have always been honorably prominent in the efforts to ameliorate the condition of their country and give it a strong nationality in which the question of religious faith should be merely incidental and unimportant. Irish Protestants are Irish, and they never had and never needed Scotch aid to fight their battles. ...

"... My people have lived in Ulster for hundreds of years, but we were never stigmatized as Scotch-Irish. We of Ulster, Protestant and Catholic, are Irish, pure and simple; and Irish nationality, undiluted by Scotch vinegar or British water, is quite good enough for us. The strength of the movement of '83 was in Ulster; the United Irish Society was formed in Ulster, and it was Irish, with no use whatever for Scotch ideas or allies ... I, as an Irishman of Ulster blood and Protestant religion, stoutly scorn this man and his Scotch-Irish rubbish. I am an Irishman, pure and simple, and I protest with vigor against my religion being used to deprive me of my nationality by this self-elected missionary. I utterly repudiate him and all his kind, and array myself under the standard of Grattan and Emmet and Parnell, and take a glorious pride in remembering that innumerable movements for Irish nationality against English misrule has been captained by Irish Protestants."

Mr. Green intimates that he is going to claim President Jackson as Irish of the prefix variety. Surely Mr. Green cannot be acquainted with the origin of the Irish Jacksons—the name coming down through the centuries from the old Milesian stock. President

Jackson himself was assuredly not afflicted with the "Scotch-Irish" heresy. Read his address at Boston, in June, 1833, to the Charitable Irish Society. On that occasion President Boyd of the Society, a Protestant, said, addressing Jackson: "Irishmen have never been backward in giving support to the institutions of this country, nor in showing due respect to the chief magistrate thereof; but when the highest office is held by the son of an Irishman, we must be allowed to indulge in some feelings of pride as well as patriotism."

To this President Jackson responded: "I feel much gratified, sir, at this testimony of respect shown me by the Charitable Irish Society of this city. It is with great pleasure that I see so many of the countrymen of my father assembled on this occasion. I have always been proud of my ancestry and of being descended from that noble race, and rejoice that I am so closely allied to a country which has so much to recommend it to the good wishes of the world. Would to God, sir, that Irishmen on the other side of the great water enjoyed the comforts, happiness and liberty they enjoy here. I am well aware, sir, that Irishmen have never been backward in giving their support to the cause of liberty. They have fought, sir, for this country valiantly, and I have no doubt would fight again were it necessary, but I hope it will be long before the institutions of our country need support of that kind. Accept my best wishes for the happiness of you all." (See records of the Society).

How the spirit of old Pat Calhoun must groan when certain writers traduce his memory by holding his son up and apart as "Scotch-Irish." In his lifetime he surely never dreamt it would come to this.

A few years since the Protestant Archbishop Plunkett of Ireland, in addressing some Presbyterian visitors, said: "I hope that while we shall always be very proud of our imperial nationality; proud of our connection with the British empire, on the history of which, as Irishmen, we have shed some lustre in the past, and from our connection with which we have derived much advantage in re-turn,—while we are proud, I say, of our imperial nationality, let us never be forgetful of our Irish nationality. We may be descended from different races—the Danes, Celts, Saxons, and Scots—but we form a combined stratum of our own, and that is Irish, and nothing else."

I cannot better extend this communication than by reproducing an extract from my original reply to Mr. Green, published in the *Boston Traveller:* An Episcopalian friend once said to me: "I notice that so long as an Irishman in this country goes to the Roman Catholic church, he is spoken of as Irish; but should he change his creed and frequent the Baptist or the Methodist church, he is im-mediately referred to by his new friends as "Scotch-Irish." This is a fair specimen of the shaky ground on which the shibboleth rests.

Touching upon the subject of Sarah Alexander, mother of the hero of Lake Erie, I ask Mr. Green if he would consider himself any the less an American because his grandfather happened to be English or Irish or Scotch? He avoids a direct answer to this, and good-naturedly brushes the question aside. So I must repeat it.

Mr. Green facetiously remarks that he might be able to estab-lish a few Scottish ancestors for myself. I think not. The Murrays (Irish, O'Muiredhaigh) are in origin Irish of the Irish. They trace descent back many centuries and at different periods have been dynasts in Cork, Meath, Derry, Mayo and other districts. They are kin to the O'Mahoneys, McCarthys and other historic Irish septs. So you see, Mr. Green, how hopeless your task would be.

Speaking of the name borne by my correspondent, I have known sturdy, full-blooded Irishmen, right from Cork and Galway, who were named both Green and Greene. Did time allow, perhaps I could trace Irish descent on the part of the distinguished librarian. I am sure he would be pleased to have me do so.

As I stated in a former letter, this "Scotch-Irish" fad has, in very truth, become an unutterable bore. While some Irish people of immediate or remote Scottish descent did unquestionably come to these shores, not five per cent. of those claimed as such by current writers were really of Scotch extraction. And these were so hopelessly overwhelmed in numbers by other Irish who came that any attempt to claim exclusive merit for the handful can only result in mortification to the claimant.

The part the Irish—the "mere Irish"—took in our revolutionary war is safely recorded in American history. "You have lost America by the Irish!" exclaimed Lord Mountjoy (1783) in the British parliament. Loyalist Galloway when questioned in the Commons as to the composition of our patriot army, replied: "I can answer the question with precision. They were scarcely one-fourth natives of America, about one-half Irish, the other fourth English and Scotch." Ramsey declares "the Irish in America were almost to a man on the side of independence," and Plowden says that many of the successes of the patriots "were immediately owing to the vigorous exertions and prowess of the Irish emigrants who bore arms in that cause."

The precious "Scotch-Irish" of modern times had not yet eventuated, it would appear. I cannot close this letter more appropriately than by quoting the tribute of Washington's adopted son, G. W. P. Custis, who thus speaks of the plain, every day Irish:—

"Then honored be the old and good services of the sons of Erin in the war of independence. Let the shamrock be entwined with the laurels of the revolution, and truth and justice guiding the pen of history inscribe on the tablets of America's remembrance, eternal gratitude to Irishmen."

THOMAS HAMILTON MURRAY.
LAWRENCE, MASS., July 6, 1895.

The correspondence closed with the following letter from Mr. Green in *The Worcester Daily Telegram* of July 9, 1895:

To the Editor of *The Telegram:*—

Mr. Murray in his rejoinder, this morning, to my reply to his recent communication, says that after a certain statement which I had made in the reply, which he quotes, and, in his use of our language, calls an "admission," "very little remains to be said."

He will therefore excuse me if, with a great deal of work crowding on me, I answer his last letter briefly, and, without agreeing with or disputing the assertions made by him regarding the general subject of what he would call the Scotch-Irish myth, merely reply to a question to which he says I avoided "a direct answer," and write a few words in defence of Hon. Leonard A. Morrison.

Mr. Murray writes: "I ask Mr. Green if he would consider himself any the less an American because his grandfather happened to be English or Irish or Scotch."

I had supposed that I had made my answer clear, but, as I do not seem to have been understood, I state distinctly that, under the circumstances mentioned, I should not consider myself any the less an American.

I will add that, under the same circumstances, I should feel at perfect liberty, did I so choose, to call myself an English-American, Irish-American or a Scotch-American, and that I do not believe I should resent it if my friends and acquaintances spoke of me in that way. It is natural and pleasant for many Americans to have the love which they bear the lands of their birth or of their ancestors recognized by an appropriate adjective before the name of the beloved country to which they now belong.

Mr. Murray seems to think that Mr. Morrison and all other persons who choose to be known as Scotch-Irish are ashamed of the name Irish.

Is that true? I am sure it is not.

If they wish to avoid being known as Irishmen, why do they not call themselves Scotchmen? Many of them I am sure, feel that while they retained the characteristics of Scotchmen, while living in Ireland, they also gained much by coming in contact with the people of Ireland.

Mr. Morrison is a student of the history of the North of Ireland, and is very proud of being descended from ancestors who lived there. He knows, of course, as do Mr. Linehan and I, that, according to the old traditions, emigrants from Ireland settled Scotland and gave it its name. But he believes, and I believe, that the mixture of races, as they were to be found in the lowlands of Scotland, from which the large colonies went into Ireland in the 17th century, was very different from the mixture of races to be found among the Irish of the same period. Mr. Linehan would probably deny this statement, but I think that people generally who have read of Scotchmen and Irishmen, or who have come in contact with them, believe that the two races differed widely during the century under consideration, and that the differences in race characteristics which showed themselves then are very obvious now.

SAMUEL SWETT GREEN.

12 Harvard street, July 8, 1895.

www.ingramcontent.com/pod-product-compliance
Lightning Source LLC
Chambersburg PA
CBHW071835020426
42331CB00007B/1735